KU-155-000

GLOBETROTTER
TRAVEL GUIDE

Sydney

BRUCE ELDER

NEW
HOLLAND

GLOBETROTTER

TRAVEL GUIDE

First edition published in 1996
by New Holland (Publishers) Ltd.
Sydney • London • Cape Town • Singapore

3/2 Aquatic Drive
Frenchs Forest NSW 2086
Australia

24 Nutford Place
London W1H 6DQ
United Kingdom

80 McKenzie Street
Cape Town 8001
South Africa

Copyright © 1996 in text: Bruce Elder
Copyright © 1996 in maps: Globetrotter Travel Maps
Copyright © 1996 in photographs:
Individual photographers as credited
Copyright © 1996 New Holland (Publishers) Ltd

ISBN 1 85368 548 8

Commissioning Publisher: Sally Bird
Managing Editor: Sean Fraser
Editor: Joanne Holliman
Design and DTP: Sonya Cupido
Cartographer: William Smuts
Compiler/Verifier: Elaine Fick
Reproduction by cmyk prepress (Pty) Ltd, Cape Town
Printed and bound in Hong Kong by South China
Printing Company (1988) Limited

Photographic Credits:
Atkins & Atkins Advertising, page 65; *Compliments
of* **Debbie Finn Publicity,** page 83; **Ian Lever,** pages
15, 52, 79 (bottom); **New Holland Australia Image
Library:** pages 66, 99, 101, 103, 111 (top), 113, *NHAIL
(Shaen Adey):* cover (bottom left), title page, pages 8,
9, 12, 18, 19, 20, 24, 40, 54 (top and bottom), 67, 74,
110, 112, *NHAIL (Arne Falkenmire):* page 102, *NHAIL
(Vicki Hastrich):* page 107, *NHAIL (Anthony Johnson):*
cover (top right and bottom right), pages 7, 10, 13,
26, 28 (bottom), 30–34, 37, 41, 43, 44, 47, 51 (top),
56, 60, 68–72, 75, 77, 78, 79 (top), 111 (bottom), 114,
NHAIL (Nick Rains): cover (top left), pages 4, 6, 11,
14, 16, 17, 21, 25, 28 (top), 35, 38, 39, 46, 48, 49, 50,
51 (bottom), 53, 58, 59, 62, 64, 73, 76, 81, 82, 84–98,
100, 104; **Nick Rains,** pages 22, 106, 109.
[NHAIL: New Holland Australia Image Library]

Cover Photographs:
Top left: *Sydney Harbour Bridge has provided
a vital link between the northern and southern
suburbs for over 50 years.*
Top right: *The stunning Sydney Opera House marks
an architectural feat and is a top tourist attraction.*
Bottom left: *Sydney has a necklace of more than
20 excellent beaches which are ideal for swimming,
surfing and relaxing.*
Bottom right: *Darling Harbour, opened during
Sydney's bicentenary, offers visitors wonderful
shopping, eating and entertainment venues.*
Title Page: *Sydney loves to party and each year a
spectacular fireworks display heralds in the New Year.*

CONTENTS

1
Introducing Sydney

Ask any Sydneysider and, whether they have travelled overseas or not, they will tell you that Sydney is one of the world's most beautiful cities. Ask them why, and they will point to the harbour which, on a sunny day, glistens and sparkles like crushed diamonds. They will point to the walks around the harbour foreshores, the natural vantage points where spectacular views can be enjoyed, the ferries that crisscross the harbour offering commuters a delightful journey to work, the parks and gardens where people walk and relax, the architectural magic of the **Harbour Bridge** and the **Opera House**, the great day trips that can be effortlessly made from the city centre, and the warmth and friendliness of the inhabitants.

But the visitor does not have to rely on Sydneysiders for glowing descriptions of this remarkable city. The English writer Anthony Trollope, when he visited Australia in the 19th century, wrote of Sydney: 'I despair of being able to convey to any reader my own idea of the beauty of **Sydney Harbour**. I have seen nothing to equal it in the way of land-locked sea scenery.'

Sir Arthur Conan Doyle, the creator of Sherlock Holmes, observed: 'The splendid landlocked bay with its numerous side estuaries and its narrow entrance is a grand playground for a sea-loving race. On a Saturday it is covered with every kind of craft, from canoe to hundred-tonner', and, in 1895, the American writer, Mark Twain, described the harbour as 'the darling of Sydney and the wonder of the world.'

TOP ATTRACTIONS

*** Sydney Opera House: one of the most remarkable buildings of the 20th century and a major attraction for visitors.
*** The Harbour's Heads: both North and South Head offer superb views of the city.
*** Taronga Park Zoo: located on the harbour foreshore, it is one of the world's finest zoos.
*** Blue Mountains: not to be missed. Dramatic scenery – sheer cliffs, wooded valleys, waterfalls and bush walks.

Opposite: *A restored ferry moored at Darling Harbour with Sydney's central business district glowing in the early evening light.*

FACTS AND FIGURES

• Sydney's **population**
in 1993 was 3,713,200.
This represented 61.9% of
the population of New South
Wales. It is Australia's most
populous city.
• The **tallest building** in the
southern hemisphere is the
Sydney Tower at Centrepoint
which is 324.8m (1065ft)
above sea level.
• **Oldest daily newspaper**
in the southern hemisphere,
the *Sydney Morning Herald*,
was established in 1831.
• The annual **Sydney Gay
& Lesbian Mardi Gras**, held
in late February, attracts the
largest crowds of any regular
public event in Australia.
In recent years, crowds
have topped 500,000.
• Sydney consumes 655,000
megalitres of water per year.
• Sydney is 869km (540
miles) from Melbourne
and 967km (600 miles)
from Brisbane by road.

THE LAND

The best way to understand the greater Sydney region is to think of it as a huge saucer-like bowl with drowned river valleys in the north (the **Hawkesbury River–Broken Bay** area), the south (**Port Hacking**) and in the middle (**Sydney Harbour**). These three fine waterways were formed during the last ice age when the sea was more than 100m (330ft) lower than its current level. When the sea level rose the river valleys were drowned. These drowned valleys can be easily seen if you fly over the city.

To the east of Sydney a series of dramatic cliffs rise from the Pacific Ocean. The rocky outcrops, known as **North Head** and **South Head**, stand like sentinels at the entrance to the harbour. These cliffs rise again in the **Royal National Park** to the south and along the coast beyond Broken Bay in the north. These sandstone outcrops form plateaux to the north and south of the city, but the centre of the greater metropolitan area is a low-lying plain which stretches west for nearly 50km (30 miles) until it reaches the Lapstone monocline at the eastern edge of the **Blue Mountains**. The westerly extremity of the city is drained by the Nepean River which flows along the base of the Blue Mountains and joins the Hawkesbury River near Windsor. In turn, the Hawkesbury cuts a valle until it reaches the sea at Broken Bay.

Right: *It takes only 15 minutes for the Jetcat to travel from Manly to Circular Quay. The inexpensive journey offers visitors excellent views of Sydney Harbour. Here the ferry cuts across the harbour opening near South Head.*

Left: *A necklace of beaches stretches from Cronulla in the south to Palm Beach in the north and include the world-famous Bondi and Manly beaches. Dee Why beach to the north shows the wide sandy shore and excellent surf typical of these ocean beaches.*

There are various points around the city (on the ridge to the south of Sutherland and along the north shore ridge between Lindfield and Pymble) where this saucer-like shape of the greater metropolitan area is evident. In both places, on a clear day, the Blue Mountains can be seen to the west of the city.

Seas and Shores

Sydney is justifiably famous for its coastline and harbour shoreline. The city's ocean coast (which stretches from Broken Bay in the north to Port Hacking in the south) is characterised by stunning beaches (like Bondi and Manly which have international reputations) set between low-lying headlands which are popular haunts for fishermen. To the north and south of the entrance to Sydney Harbour the more than 20 excellent beaches are ideal for swimming, surfing, sunbaking and relaxing during the summer months, and perfect for picnics and walks during the cooler months.

Large areas of the shoreline of the harbour have been retained in public ownership with numerous walking tracks around the headlands and along the harbour beaches. Each area of the harbour has its most popular beach. On the northside Balmoral, Clontarf and Clifton Gardens are popular haunts while both Camp Cove and Neilsen's Park are popular harbour beaches serving the city's Eastern Suburbs.

BEST BEACHES

Every Sydney beach has its own particular attractions.
*** Bondi Beach: a very popular and beautiful stretch of sand easily accessible from the city centre.
*** Whale Beach: difficult to access but worth the effort; a quiet beach inhabited by the city's rich and famous.
*** Manly Beach: actually a series of beaches; accessible from the city by ferry and bus.
*** Palm Beach: this beach is ideal for walks; it has a non-suburban feel.

CLIMATE

Sydneysiders feel that they live in a city with a perfect climate. The summers are usually long and sunny, but, if there are cyclones off the Queensland coast, the city can experience extended periods of summer rain. It is also common to have summer storms, and the city's famous 'southerly buster' – a dramatic cold change often after particularly hot and humid days – is a feature of hot summers that can send temperatures tumbling. The winters are mild, although snow does occasionally fall in the Blue Mountains and on the Southern Highlands.

Climate

Sydney is a city of mild temperatures, evenly distributed rainfall with slight maximums in the late autumn and early winter, and glorious, balmy, subtropical summer days of sunshine. The sun shines on an average of 342 days a year. The greater metropolitan area, which now spreads about 25km (15 miles) to the south, 35km (20 miles) to the north, and over 50km (30 miles) to the west and south-west, experiences considerable variation. It is common for the outer western and southwestern suburbs to experience frosts in the winter and to be up to 5C° (9F°) warmer in summer. The upper north shore offers spectacular autumnal displays as the leaves on the deciduous trees change colour, and both the **Blue Mountains** and **Southern Tablelands** are regularly brushed by light snowfalls during the winter months.

Plant Life

The enduring image of Sydney and its environs is the **eucalypt**, gum tree. This tree is characteristic of the entire Sydney basin. In its most beautiful manifestation, in the Blue Mountains to the west of Sydney, it gives the appearance of being lightly brushed with a smoky blue. At its worst, on the poor sandstone soils to the south of the city, it appears as a shabby grey-green foliage which is both useless and unattractive.

Extensive planting of deciduous European trees has meant that many of the suburban areas (particularly those areas on the city's upper north shore) look European rather than Australian.

Wildlife

Sydney has been settled by Europeans for over 200 years and consequently the wildlife has been marginalised and is rarely seen outside the city's zoo and the nature reserves.

While distinctive Australian animals such as the **koala**, **platypus**, **kangaroo**, **wallaby** and **spiny anteater** once lived in the area, they are rarely seen today.

Monotremes (egg-laying mammals), such as the **platypus** and **echidna** (spiny anteater), and marsupials – ranging from **kangaroos** and **wallabies** to **wombats** and **koalas** – may be seen in the wild, but are more common in zoos and wildlife parks.

In the bushland areas around Sydney, **snakes** and **spiders** are common. Sydney's sandstone is home to the **funnelweb spider** (a particularly aggressive and poisonous variety of spider which is well worth avoiding) and the **redback**, a relative of the North American black widow, can be found in dark holes and corners.

There is a popular perception, however, that Sydney is full of dangerous creatures: deadly redback and funnel-webspiders, large numbers of poisonous snakes and seas teeming with sharks and deadly blue-ringed octopii. This is not an accurate perception. In fact Australia, with the exception of the dingo, has no land-based carnivores. Consequently, one of the greatest problems is that intro-duced species – notably feral varieties of domestic dogs and cats – have, in recent years, caused havoc with native species of birds and smaller mammals which have spent thousands of years living without natural predators.

The most common wildlife seen in the Sydney area are the birds. Bushwalkers are likely to see numerous **magpies** and the occasional brightly coloured **lorikeet**. In the city **pigeons** and **sparrows** are abundant, and people visiting beaches will find the ubiquitous **seagull** competing with the occasional **pelican**.

Above: *Koalas are rarely seen in the wild in Sydney, but they can be found at the zoo or in wildlife parks.*
Opposite: *The* Angophora costata, *with its gnarled pink trunk and branches, is common in Sydney.*

DEADLY CREATURES

Sydney has many spiders. Two are quite common and are capable of biting and poisoning human beings. The **funnelweb**, found throughout the Sydney basin, is ground dwelling and can live for up to five years. When attacked its fangs dribble venom and it rears up on its hind legs ready to attack. The **redback** commonly lives around domestic buildings. Its venom is dangerous to humans. People bitten by either spider should be taken to the nearest hospital.

HISTORY IN BRIEF

The history of Sydney is the history of the settlement of Australia by Europeans. Prior to the arrival of Europeans, a number of different groups of Aborigines lived around the harbour.

Captain James Cook sailed up the east coast of Australia in 1770. He entered Botany Bay and thought it suitable for a colony. He did not enter Sydney Harbour and, seeing it only from the ocean, did not recognize its unique deepwater facilities.

On 13 May 1787 a fleet of 11 vessels left Britain bound for **Botany Bay** to establish a penal colony. The flagship of the fleet, the 520 tonne *HMS Sirius*, was captained by **Arthur Phillip** who had been commissioned to become the colony's first governor. The vessels arrived at Botany Bay on the night of 19 January 1788.

HISTORICAL CALENDAR

1788 Penal colony established at Sydney Cove.
1793 First play, *The Recruiting Officer*, performed by convicts and first church built.
1803 Australia's first newspaper, *Sydney Gazette and NSW Advertiser*, published. First Roman Catholic mass held.
1804 Convicts rebel at Castle Hill near Sydney.
1826 First street lamp established in Macquarie Place.
1828 Sydney's first bank robbery. Robbers stole £12,000.
1838 World's first postage stamp used in Sydney.
1850 Australia's first university, University of Sydney, founded.
1854 Sydney Cricket Ground opened.
1855 Sydney's first railway line completed between city and Parramatta.
1863 Sections of city lit by electricity.
1881 First zoo opened. It moved to Taronga Park in 1916.
1883 First train from Sydney to Melbourne.
1901 The Commonwealth of Australia was inaugurated in Centennial Park.

1906 Central Railway Station opened.
1910 Mitchell Library opened.
1923 Two radio stations – 2SB and 2FC – started broadcasting. Construction started on Sydney's underground railway.
1930 Donald Bradman scored 452 not out in 415 minutes at the Sydney Cricket Ground.
1932 Sydney Harbour Bridge opened.
1938 200 people were swept out to sea by huge waves at Bondi Beach.
1942 Three Japanese submarines entered Sydney Harbour. The barracks ship *Kuttabul* was torpedoed.
1945 First Sydney–Hobart Yacht Race.
1946 First bikini banned from Bondi Beach.
1953 First Sydney Film Festival held.
1973 Sydney Opera House opened.
1980 Centrepoint Tower, the city's tallest building, is completed.
1988 Sydney celebrates its Bicentenary.
1992 Sydney Harbour Tunnel opened. It eases congestion on the Harbour Bridge.
1993 Sydney wins the right to host the 2000 Olympics.

Phillip quickly determined that Botany Bay, so strongly recommended by Cook for its good soils and deep grasses, was unsuitable. On 21 January, accompanied by a small detachment of marines, he rowed north in three small boats to explore **Port Jackson** and **Broken Bay**. That afternoon, Phillip entered Port Jackson. He was later to write that it was 'one of the finest harbours in the world, in which a thousand sail of the line might ride in perfect security'. Phillip landed on the northern shore of the harbour where he encountered about 20 unarmed Aborigines. Thinking them strong and friendly, he named the beach they were standing on, 'Manly'. The row boats then crossed the harbour and near the southern headland established a camp on a beach which, to this day, is called **Camp Cove**.

Phillip subsequently explored the southern shoreline, eventually finding a cove with deep mooring and a fresh stream which he named Sydney Cove, after **Lord Sydney**, the British Secretary of State at the time.

On 26 January, Phillip led the fleet north to Sydney Harbour. By the middle of the day convicts were cutting down trees around the edge of **Sydney Cove** and, as the day came to an end, Phillip and his officers raised the Union Jack of Queen Anne and toasted the British royal family and the future of the colony.

The settlement started with nothing. Houses had to be built, streets and lanes carved out of the slopes on either side of the **Tank Stream**, quarters constructed for the soldiers and convicts, fields planted and the countryside explored. This was the true and indecorous origin of Sydney: a dirty and desolate penal colony at the end of the world.

Opposite: *Sydney is a maritime city. Statues around the city celebrate the nautical achievements of both Captain James Cook (pictured here), the first European to sail up Australia's eastern coast, and Captain Arthur Phillip, who discovered the harbour and established the city.*
Below: *Hyde Park Barracks were originally built by convicts to accommodate up to 800 convicts. They are part of historic Macquarie Street and now house the Museum of Social History in New South Wales.*

Right: *One of Sydney's premier daytrip tourist attractions is the Blue Mountains west of the city. Characterized by spectacular waterfalls, dramatic cliff faces and sheer box canyons, the mountains offer a sharp contrast to the watery attractions of Sydney Harbour.*
Opposite: *The thriving city centre is linked by a monorail to Darling Harbour, which has become Sydney's premier commercial tourist attraction.*

The first years in the colony were difficult. The supplies which had been brought on the **First Fleet** were inadequate. The tools were unsuitable and the expertise of both the convicts and the soldiers was limited. The colony waited for every new ship from England, Batavia and the Cape of Good Hope. When a ship did not arrive, the colony was threatened by starvation.

Conflict between Aborigines and Europeans occurred within months of the landing. In May 1788 a convict working beyond Sydney Cove killed an Aborigine, and shortly afterwards two convicts were speared and killed while gathering rushes at the place now known as Rushcutters Bay.

By 1791, land had been granted to over 150 people in the hope that the agricultural base of the infant settlement could be broadened. Phillip pleaded with the British government to send out free settlers with farming experience so that the colony could become self-sufficient. By the mid-1790s, farms with convicts as labourers, were providing Sydney with supplies.

In the years that followed a series of governors, most of them with military or naval backgrounds, battled to solve the problems of the new colony. The great challenge, however, lay inland from Sydney. The Blue Mountains seemed impassible to the explorers who made their way across the Sydney basin. When, after

numerous attempts, they were finally crossed in 1813
by the explorers **Blaxland**, **Wentworth** and **Lawson**,
it was merely a question of time before the whole of
New South Wales was settled.

It is appropriate that this exploration milestone was
reached during the governorship of **Lachlan Macquarie**.
Macquarie, who was governor from 1810 to 1823, trans-
formed the struggling colony. During his administration,
numerous public buildings were constructed with the
help of the gifted ex-convict architect **Francis Greenway**.
Public education was introduced, treatment of women
and children was addressed, and the first bank (the
Bank of New South Wales) was granted a charter.

The history of Sydney from 1825 until the 1860s is
that of a prison slowly evolving into a society where
free settlers and emancipated convicts worked together.
The turning point occurred in May 1851 when **Edward
Hargraves** brought 120g (around 4oz) of gold to Sydney,
triggering the gold rushes. Overnight, workers in
Sydney downed tools and headed
for the goldfields and miners and
prospectors from all over the
world passed through Sydney
eager to try their luck.

The city continued to expand
throughout the 1870s and 1880s.
At times its status as Australia's
premier city was challenged by
Melbourne, but it has remained
Australia's main arrival point
and the country's financial and
industrial centre.

The post-World War II development of the city has seen enormous
changes including the construction
of the Opera House, the creation of
efficient urban transport, and the
enormous growth of suburban
Sydney so that it is now a city
similar in size to Los Angeles.

THE EARLY STRUGGLE

The 11 ships of the First Fleet
sailed into Botany Bay in
January 1788, but Captain
Phillip was disappointed
with the land and chose
Port Jackson instead. The
settlement struggled in the
early years with indifferent
land, diseases, pests, hostility
from the Aborigines, a lack
of skills, and convicts who
were not enthusiastic
workers. The arrival of the
Second Fleet in 1790 eased
the struggle somewhat, but
starvation threatened the
colony for some years. It was
not until 1808 that the first
shipment of saleable wool
was shipped to England.

GOVERNMENT AND ECONOMY

The government of Sydney is a mixture of local councils which specifically address the immediate needs of local communities, and the NSW state government which, while concerned with the total administration of the state, recognizes that over 60% of the state's population live in the Sydney area.

The NSW state

Above: *A number of Sydney's finest historic public buildings are on Macquarie Street. The NSW Parliament House, Hyde Park Barracks, Mitchell Library, Sydney Hospital and the old Sydney Mint stand as a reminder of the city's status in the history of Australia.*

government, which is located in **Parliament House** in **Macquarie Street**, Sydney, is primarily concerned with state issues. Its major areas of legislative and administrative interest include education, the police force, roads, hospitals and local health.

The city has a large number of local councils. Most are run by councillors who receive a small stipend and who make decisions about local roads, sewerage, garbage collection, planning permission and property development in the local district. They are often constrained by state and federal legislation but they do enjoy considerable power within the local community.

Historically, Sydney was a colony of Britain which was administered by a governor appointed by the British parliament. In the early years of the colony, this administration went unchallenged as a series of governors wrestled with the problems of trying to run a successful penal colony.

In 1823, Governor **Lachlan Macquarie** established the basis for the state's **Legislative Council**. It was the first move towards some kind of self-government. That same year the **Supreme Court** was given full independence and the old military rule (which had existed since 1788) began to be phased out.

As the population increased, the needs of both Sydney and New South Wales changed. During

Major-General Ralph Darling's governorship (1825–31) the colony's Legislative Council was enlarged, and government customs offices, postal services and a land office were all established.

It was now clear that the old administrative mechanisms which had kept the colony tied to the British parliament were no longer appropriate. The British handed over control of land policy to the Legislative Council in 1852 and a form of responsible government was granted when, in 1855, an elected lower house, the Legislative Assembly, was created. Sydney formally became the administrative centre for the whole state, which then encompassed the whole of the eastern seaboard.

Economic Development

In the decade from 1841 to 1861 the population of Sydney more than trebled – from 29,973 to 95,789 – as a result of the gold rushes. The rural squattocracy (a kind of colonial aristocracy) which had traditionally controlled the state and the city were now in a minority but, because of the unfair weighting of the electoral system, they still controlled both houses of parliament.

The state prospered through the 1880s and the outbreak of World War I fuelled the already buoyant economy. By 1918 Sydney and New South Wales had the strongest economic base in Australia.

Infrastructure

The success of **New South Wales** was a result of the strength and diversity of its economic base and the unchallenged position of Sydney as the financial and industrial capital of Australia.

Sydney **airport** is the primary destination for the majority of overseas flights arriving in Australia, and

---

SYDNEY HARBOUR BRIDGE

A bridge across the harbour was first mooted in the 1850s. The first known drawing of a bridge dates from 1857. In 1923 a bridge was approved by the NSW government. The tender for £4,217,721.11s. 10d was won by the engineering company Dorman Long & Co Ltd of Middlesborough, England. The technical staff came from England, the stonemasons from Scotland and the stone came from Moruya on the NSW south coast. The final cost of the bridge was £9,577,507.

Below: *Captain Arthur Phillip described Sydney Harbour as 'one of the finest harbours in the world, in which a thousand sail of the line might ride in perfect security'. He could not have imagined that it would become a place of endless recreation.*

Sydney Harbour, with the internationally recognised
Opera House and Harbour Bridge, is still regarded as
Australia's premier tourist destination.

Equally Sydney is the transportation hub for the state
of New South Wales with all major rail services arriving
and departing from Sydney's **Central Railway Station**
and the intra- and interstate bus services operating
from various points around the city.

Industry

Sydney is the economic centre of New South Wales and,
in certain industries, is the centre for the whole of Australia.
The city has also become home to the major television
networks and headquarters for most of the national media
organizations. Its **financial district** is equal to Melbourne
with many major banks and insurance companies having
their head offices in the Sydney city centre.

The city has large, definable industrial areas. Historically they have occupied the southern and western inner
suburbs but, as the city grew, they moved further to the
west and southwest. Large industrial estates are common
in areas such as **Silverwater** and **Campbelltown**.

Energy and Water

Sydney's water comes from a series of dams located on its
outskirts, of which the **Warragamba Dam** is the most well
known. These dams are located on the upper reaches of
the **Nepean** and **Woronora** rivers and utilise the steep,
narrow valleys to great effect. Although Australia regularly
experiences **drought**, it is rare for Sydney to be placed
under water restrictions. Towards the end of long drought
periods there will be restrictions on watering gardens.

The city's **energy** comes from a series of thermal and
hydro-electric power stations located throughout New
South Wales. **The Hunter Valley**, north of Sydney, is a
major supplier of coal and the power stations in the area
are part of Sydney's electricity grid. Similarly, the vast
Snowy Mountain Hydro-Electricity Scheme, which taps
the waters from the winter snows in the area, is a major
supplier of electricity to the state's grid.

Below: *Martin Place is the
centre of the city's banking
and finance district. At the
western end is the General
Post Office which opens
onto the city's cenotaph.*

Left: *Good weather and an easy-going lifestyle have seen hundreds of outdoor restaurants spring up in Sydney over the past 20 years. High-quality fresh produce and great chefs mean that eating out is one of the city's most inexpensive and delightful activities.*

THE PEOPLE

Sydneysiders like to think of themselves as friendly and gregarious. If you are lost or need help, feel free to approach someone and ask for advice. If they are unfriendly, they are the exception not the rule.

Visitors used to societies which are aggressively driven by customer service may find that service, particularly in shops, hotels and in the tourist trade, is lax and informal. **Sydneysiders** do not like to see themselves as aggressive. This may come as a surprise to visitors who find that the linguistic tendency to finish a sentence on a rising note sounds abrasive and questioning.

It is important always to remember the roots of Sydney society. The European community in Sydney was almost totally **Anglo-Saxon** until the 1950s. The resistance to overseas and multicultural impulses was so strong that the arrival of large numbers of **Chinese** on the goldfields of New South Wales in the 1850s and 1860s led to riots. There was, for nearly a century, an informal policy, which was dubbed 'the White Australia Policy', that made entry into the country for non-Anglo-Saxons very difficult, indeed nearly impossible.

This resistance to non-Anglo influences resulted in a narrow cuisine, open and sustained racist antagonism towards the **Aborigines**, and a belief that the country was in threat of being overrun by hordes of outsiders.

SYDNEY'S BICENTENARY

On 26 January 1788, Sydney Cove became Australia's first European settlement when 11 ships carrying 736 convicts arrived from England. Two hundred years later over 2 million people stood on the shores of Sydney Harbour to watch the Bicentenary celebrations. Prince Charles and Princess Diana were the special guests. The day included a First Fleet re-enactment, a parade of Tall Ships, an air-force flyover and a fireworks display. Aborigines protested 200 years of European domination. Over 1 million people inspected the Tall Ships while they were moored in Sydney.

Above: *Although Sydney's Aboriginal communities are plagued by unemployment, they have set up important cultural centres with dance companies, legal services and education facilities.*

MUSEUM OF SYDNEY

Located on the site of the city's first Government House (the corner of Bridge and Phillip streets) the Museum of Sydney provides visitors with an excellent insight into the city's history. At the entrance is the original 1788 sandstone foundation to Governor Phillip's first residence. There is a floor devoted to the story of the Eora people who lived in the Sydney basin before the arrival of the Europeans. Another floor depicts Sydney's history from 1788–1850 and there are panoramas depicting the changes from settlement to the present day.

Most Sydneysiders are proud of the country's **convict heritage.** Jokes about the society being a collection of descendants of convicts are, however, now totally inacurate. They can be rebutted by proud declarations that Sydney is a very egalitarian society which is based on personal success and whether you are a decent and worthwhile human being.

Sydneysiders are much like all Australians: there is a great acceptance of achievement matched with humility and a great intolerance of achievement when it is associated with flashy vulgarity.

There is still, in some sectors of Sydney's society, a perceived division between the 'workers' and the 'bosses': the 'them and us' syndrome. One theory argues that this dates back to convict times when relationships between convicts and overseers were similarly antagonistic.

Sydney's weather ensures a sense of relaxed informality. Some visitors have remarked that in summer Sydney looks as though everyone is on holiday: men wear shorts and women wear light, summer frocks. This informality even extends to the more expensive restaurants and hotels where open-necked shirts and casual clothing (although not rubber sandals and sleeveless T-shirts) are acceptable.

The Aboriginal Society

Like all big cities Sydney draws people from rural areas. Many **Aborigines** gravitate to Sydney and, while many are integrated into the larger community, there is a substantial Aboriginal community in the inner city suburb of **Redfern**. Today Redfern is the home of a variety of facilities and services including the famous **Bangarra Dance Theatre**, and offices like the **Aboriginal Legal Centre**, are located in the area.

The Aborigines in the southern suburb of **La Perouse** can trace their roots back to pre-European settlement. Each year, on 26 January (**Australia Day**), they gather in one of the area's large parks to celebrate their survival since the arrival of Europeans.

In recent times Aborigines, who for most of the country's European history have been treated appallingly, have asserted their rights. This hardly redresses the long period of imbalance when they were poisoned, massacred, driven from their land, forced into reserves, treated as social outcasts and had their families torn apart by bureaucratic wrong-headedness.

During the 1990s major changes have occurred and the potential conditions of Aborigines have improved. Perhaps the most significant change occurred in 1994 when the Federal Government converted the High Court's 'Mabo' decision into legislation. This legislation, which was a long and complex document, basically stated that if Aborigines could prove continuous connection with the land, they could under most circumstances claim that land as their own. This reversed the famous *terra nullius* proposition which was created when **Captain Cook** stood on Cape York and, in spite of seeing signs of human inhabitants all along the country's east coast, declared that Australia was uninhabited and, therefore, it could legitimately be claimed by the British Crown.

> **THE ABORIGINES**
>
> If you are interested in learning more about Sydney's Aborigines, there are two excellent books available. Keith Willey's *When the Sky Fell Down: The Destruction of the Tribes of the Sydney Region 1788–1850s* (Collins, Sydney, 1979) is a detailed history of the impact of the European settlement on the area, and Eric Willmot's *Pemulwuy: The Rainbow Warrior* (Weldon, Sydney, 1987) is an excellent account of one of the most famous leaders the Aboriginal resistance in the Sydney basin.

Left: *Australia Day is celebrated on 26 January. This summertime public holiday is celebrated informally at beaches, in local parks and, in the centre, at the plazas and parks where people gather to enjoy free entertainment.*

Right: *Sydney's Gay and Lesbian Mardi Gras attracts tourists from all over the world. It is a celebration of gay pride. These drag queens at the 1996 Mardi Gras symbolise the joy and good humour which characterize the event.*

Language and Culture

After **World War II** Australia embarked on an active immigration programme. It is probable that this programme was driven by fear, exacerbated by the Japanese invasion of northern Australia during the war, combined with a desire to settle refugees from the war in Europe. Many of these migrants settled in Sydney resulting in dramatic changes in the language and culture of the city. Where it was once Anglo-Saxon, now it is a truly **multicultural society**. Since 1945 it has experienced constant migrations – first from Eastern Europe, then in the 1950s from Britain, Greece and Italy, then later from Turkey and the Lebanon and, most recently, from Southeast Asia, particularly Vietnam and Hong Kong.

While many immigrants have adopted the Australian way of life, there are still areas of the city characterized by dominant ethnic cultures. Cabramatta, in Sydney's west, has a large **Vietnamese** community and the main street has numerous Vietnamese restaurants and food shops. Similarly, Leichhardt is predominantly **Italian**; Newtown and Enmore still have significant **Greek** communities; Granville has many **Lebanese** and **Turks**; and Liverpool has a substantial **Indian** community.

JAPANESE SUBMARINES IN SYDNEY HARBOUR

On 31 May 1942 three midget Japanese submarines attempted to enter Sydney Harbour. One submarine got caught in an anti-torpedo net and blew itself up. Another fired two torpedoes at the USS *Chicago* which was moored in the harbour, and the third hit the harbour floor, exploded and blew a hole in the HMAS *Kuttabul*, killing 19 Australian and two British sailors. While the two submarines which had exploded were retrieved from the bottom of the harbour, the third got away. The parent submarine stayed in the waters outside the harbour and sunk three coastal ships in the next 10 days.

The inevitable cultural domination of the **United States** has changed the country's language (to a point where most people would now spell 'gaol' as 'jail'), the clothing fashions of baseball and basketball have become defining fashion statements for teenagers, American movies dominate in the major cinema complexes, and the all-pervasive US fast food empires – McDonalds, Pizza Hut and KFC – have become an integral part of Sydney's eating habits.

Modern Sydney suburbia is remarkably similar to American suburbia with large shopping complexes, huge parking lots, the majority of people driving their own cars, freeways abound and most people live in single-storey brick bungalows on neat suburban plots.

Religion

Sydney, like much of Australia, is predominantly **Christian**. Each suburb in the city is likely to have churches representing the major Christian faiths (**Anglican**, **Roman Catholic**, **Uniting** – a combination of **Presbyterians** and **Methodists**) as well as minority faiths including the **Church of the Latter Day Saints**, various ethnic Orthodox churches (**Greek Orthodox** is particularly strong) and **Baptists**.

Where once Sydney only had Christian churches, now it is common to see **Buddhist** temples and **Muslim** mosques. In Wollongong, for example, the largest religious building in the city is a Buddhist temple; and in Granville, in Sydney's western suburbs, an Imam calls the faithful to prayer from the tower of an elegant, modern mosque. By 1986 Australia had nearly 110,000 practising **Muslims**, over 80,000 **Buddhists**, nearly 70,000 practising **Jews** and 21,500 **Hindus**, many of whom lived in Sydney.

Below: *The Fokuangshan Nan Tien Buddhist Temple south of Wollongong is the largest Buddhist temple in the southern hemisphere.*

Above: *The hugely popular annual Opera in the Park concert attracts as many as 100,000 concert-goers from all walks of life.*

The Arts

Sydney's cultural life has changed dramatically in the past 50 years. From a narrow cultural world based on the proposition that everything from the UK was good and everything in Australia was second-rate, there has been a growing sense of national pride. Today Sydneysiders are proud of their rich and diverse culture.

There is still a tendency to take great pride in overseas recognition of Australian achievement. Thus **Patrick White** (who won the Nobel Prize for Literature) and **Thomas Keneally** and **Peter Carey** (who have both won the Booker Prize) are lionised as the city's greatest writers. This is a vast improvement on the situation when a professor of literature in the 1950s, declared that there was no such thing as Australian literature, and that **D.H. Lawrence's** novel *Kangaroo* (which is still a marvellous evocation of Sydney) was the best the country could offer.

The literary situation has been closely followed by the success of Australian films. The success of Jane Campion's *The Piano* (although Campion herself is actually a New Zealander) was greeted enthusiastically and the success of **Peter Weir**, cinematographer **Dean Semmler** (who won an Oscar for his work on *Dances With Wolves*), **Fred Schepisi** and **Bruce Bereseford** has received wide local attention.

Sydney has a healthy high art scene. The **Sydney Symphony Orchestra** is of international standing. Sydney's opera singers (most notably **Joan Sutherland** and **Yvonne Kenny**) have starred in the world's great opera houses. Sydney's ballet companies and dance troupes receive international acclaim and local painters and artists (notably the late **Brett Whiteley**) celebrated the city's beauty and are represented in the world's great art collections and galleries.

Of course the day-to-day cultural reality for the average Sydneysider is markedly different. The love of sport, the fascination with television, the unswerving desire to have a good time, is a vital aspect of the city's culture. Many outdoor activities are held, including the popular domain concerts. These free concerts are held in January each year in conjunction with the Sydney Arts Festival. As many as 100,000 people attend the Symphony Under the Stars, Australia Day and Opera in the Park concerts.

Sport and Recreation

With a pleasant climate and numerous outdoor facilities, Sydney can be seen as a sports-mad city. In many instances, it is hard to define what is a major sport and what is a minor one. Clearly in summertime the pre-eminent sport is **cricket**. There is a suburban first-grade competition from which players can be chosen for the **NSW Sheffield Shield** state side. There are also numerous lower levels of competition. It is still quite common to see people playing a friendly game of informal cricket under sunny skies in the streets of the neighbourhood or the local park.

SYDNEY 2000 OLYMPICS

The 2000 Olympics will be held in Sydney. For the first time in modern Olympic history the 15,000 participating athletes and officials will be housed in a single Olympic Village. Most of the events will be held at Sydney Olympic Park which will include an Olympic Stadium (capacity 80,000), an Aquatic Centre (12,400), Sports Centre (4500), Auditorium (15,000), Hockey Centre (15,000), Tennis Centre (10,000), and Baseball Centre (10,000). Sailing events will be held on Sydney Harbour.

Below: *Located 14km (19 miles) from the centre of Sydney, the Sydney Olympic Park is being built as the venue for the 2000 Olympics.*

WORLD CRICKET

In the 1970s the Sydney businessman, **Kerry Packer**, created a rebel cricket competition which was shown exclusively on his television network, **Channel 9**. This evolved into a series of competitions known variously as **World Series Cricket** and the **World Cup**. Both competitions are played in one day with each side batting and bowling for a maximum of 50 overs. It has become extremely popular as it is much faster and more exciting than the usual five-day International Test.

While first grade cricket matches often have rather poor attendances, international matches at the **Sydney Cricket Ground** (and friendly internationals at the **Bradman Oval** in Bowral) and one-day cricket attract huge crowds.

The other major summer sport is swimming. Again, this ranges from regular suburban and state competitions through to the people who swim a few laps before or after work. Facilities throughout the city are excellent – and a number of suburban backyards boast swimming pools.

In winter, Sydneysiders play rugby union, rugby league, soccer and netball. Major competitions are fiercely competitive and are commonly broadcast on radio and television. Although no-one likes to admit it, there are clear social divisions which attach to the football codes. Rugby union is still a predominantly middle class activity. It draws the bulk of its players from the city's private school competitions. Rugby league, the largest football code in the city, is more overtly working class and soccer is popular with the large European immigrant community, particularly the British, Italians and peoples from the Balkan states.

The strength of Sydney sport lies more in the number of people who play than the number of people who watch. On any Saturday, in any reasonably sized suburb, there will be competitions at the local golf course, on the netball courts, and on the cricket and football fields. Beyond these competitions there is a large amount of recreational fishing,

Below: *The Sydney Cricket Ground is the venue for international matches in Sydney.*

bushwalking, swimming, and – of course – surfing. It is also common for outdoor picnics and barbecues to be accompanied by a friendly game of touch football, French cricket or some similarly energetic sport.

It is somewhat of a cliché to see Australians as sports-obsessed but there is more than an element of truth. Participation rates are high and, as a social activity, sport attracts millions of people every weekend.

Food and Drink

There was a time, still celebrated on the national airline, Qantas, when breakfast consisted of a piece steak, fried tomatoes and eggs. Equally, there was a time when an invitation on either a Saturday or Sunday lunchtime would ensure that the barbecue would be lit and sausages and steaks would be cooked.

Above: *Some of the country's finest wines originate in the cellars of the Hunter Valley.*

The accompanying tomato sauce, bread and butter, salad with no dressing and a rice salad (washed down with beer for the men and shandies or wine for the women) were part of the fabric of Sydney's weekend entertainment.

While these activities are still regular features of Sydney life, concern about calorie intake, a more ascetic approach to food, and the increasing variety of foods available as a result of the country's increasing multiculturalism, have meant that these clichés are no longer mandatory.

It is quite likely that beer at the barbecue has been replaced by a fine wine from the **Hunter Valley**, the **Barossa Valley** or the **Margaret River** area of Western Australia. The usual sauces may well have given way to something more exotic from Asia. The steak and sausage barbecue will often see prawns, pieces of fish and chicken replacing the heavier red meats.

Sydneysiders eat and drink well. They are able to do so because they have a high standard of living and because the country's produce is of high quality, is readily available and is, by world standards, very cheap. Most visitors are surprised at how inexpensive – and fresh – food is.

Sydneysiders enjoy the city's excellent wine bars and coffee lounges. They range widely across the city's diverse ethnic restaurants, displaying an easy tolerance towards the diverse cuisine which has so significantly altered the city's lifestyle over the past 50 years.

PADDY'S MARKET

Every Sydneysider remembers the original Paddy's Market with great affection. The pace of modern change, and the need to modernise the city, forced stallholders away from the city centre and they were temporarily relocated at Redfern, west of the city centre. In recent times, Paddy's Market has returned to the edge of Chinatown. It is Sydney's biggest market market with over 1000 stalls selling everything from footwear to jewellery, toys to Australian souvenirs. The market is well worth visiting. Open Saturday and Sunday, 09:00–16:30. Paddy's Info Hotline, tel: 11589.

2
Central Sydney

Sydney's Central Business District lies south of the harbour and is rich in history. Against a backdrop of water visitors can walk across the Harbour Bridge, explore The Rocks and Circular Quay, wander through the Botanic Gardens, inspect Macquarie Street's historic buildings, and shop in the city centre and Darling Harbour.

THE BEST OF SYDNEY
The Harbour Bridge ★★★
No visit to Sydney is complete without a leisurely walk across the Sydney Harbour Bridge. To reach the pedestrian walkway, walk up Argyle Street in The Rocks, climb the Argyle Steps, cross Cumberland Street and follow the signs marked 'Bridge Stairs'. The view is spectacular at any time of the day but is particularly impressive in the early morning or late afternoon.

The bridge is Australia's most famous and distinctive construction. It took nine years to build, weighs 60,000 tonnes and, at its highest point, is 134m (440ft) above the harbour. It is listed in the *Guinness Book of Records* as the widest steel arch bridge in the world with eight traffic lanes, two railway lines, a cycleway and footway all being located on a deck which is 49m (160ft) wide.

The harbour has always been a natural barrier between north and south, and the Sydney Harbour Bridge forms a link between the city's northern and southern suburbs.

At the time of the bridge's opening it cost six pence per passenger in a car to cross. Today it costs $2 when travelling from the north side and is free from the south.

DON'T MISS

★★★ The Rocks: an excellent mixture of history and tourism. Try to imagine the hardships of the early settlers of Sydney.
★★★ Sydney Aquarium: a truly comprehensive overview of Australia's freshwater and saltwater fish.
★★★ Royal Botanic Gardens: escape from the concrete and steel of Sydney and appreciate the beauty of the harbour.
★★★ Opera House and Centrepoint Tower: both are outstanding attractions.

Opposite: *The Sydney Harbour Bridge links the north and south shores of the city's harbour.*

Above: Once dangerous and wild, The Rocks has become one of the city's most popular tourist haunts.
Below: Cadman's Cottage is Sydney's oldest building. Ex-convict, John Cadman, lived in this modest stone cottage for 30 years between 1816–46.

The Rocks **

Although now predominantly a tourist attraction with historic pubs, restaurants and chic gift shops, this was the centre of the city's wild military and convict nightlife in the 18th and 19th centuries, and remains Sydney's most historically significant area.

An ideal walk through The Rocks starts on George Street at the Cahill Expressway, moves down to the **Mercantile Hotel**, turns back along the walkway below Cumberland Street, descends the stairs at the **Argyle Cut** and cuts back through Playfair Street to the **Rocks Square**. This could take as little as half an hour, would include the old **Police Station** (1882) on the western side of George Street, the **Museum of Contemporary Art** over the road, and **John Cadman's cottage** (1816 – Sydney's oldest building) next door to **The Rocks Visitors Centre** (open 09:00 to 17:00 daily) which is located in the old **Sailors' Home**.

Further along, on the Quay side of George Street, steps lead down to the **Mariners' Church** (1856) and the **ASN Co building** (1884). Further along George Street, past the Old Sydney Park Royal Hotel, there is the **Merchants House Museum** on the left and impressive stores on the right which contain **The Rocks Weekend Market**. Turning the corner at the Mercantile Hotel there is a pleasant walk back to the **Argyle Steps** which go down to the **Argyle Centre** and **The Rocks Centre**.

There are a many free shows, interesting galleries (particularly the **Aboriginal Art and Tribal Centre** at 117 George Street and the **S.H. Ervin Gallery** on Observatory Hill), and shops specializing in opals, Australian memorabilia and toy Australian animals.

Circular Quay ★★★

Circular Quay, previously known as Sydney Cove, was the centre of the first European colony and it is still the place where Sydneysiders congregate to celebrate Australia Day, the country's Bicentenary (in 1988) or the winning of the 2000 Olympics bid.

On a warm, sunny day take an idle stroll around the cove. Start at the **Park Hyatt Sydney Hotel** on the western edge near the bridge and wander along the foreshore to **Campbells Storehouse** (1839–61). You might like to stop at one of the restaurants offering seafood, Italian and Chinese cuisine, and indigenous Australian meals. Lying at anchor in **Campbells Cove** is the *Bounty*, a faithful replica of Captain Bligh's 18th-century vessel which was built for the Mel Gibson film *Mutiny on the Bounty*.

As you round the corner into Sydney Cove you may see a cruise ship at the International Terminal. Beyond lies the gracious sandstone **Customs House**, now converted into the **Museum of Contemporary Art**. It has travelling exhibitions as well as an excellent permanent collection of important international contemporary artworks.

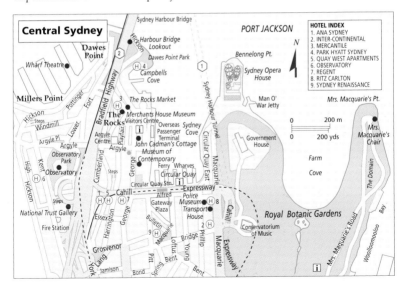

Circular Quay has a number of ferry services to Manly, Taronga Park Zoo, Cremorne Point, Mosman, Neutral Bay, Darling Harbour, Balmain and many other destinations. If you have enough time, make a special attempt to take a return trip on one of the ferries. It may not be an organized tour, but it is a delightful way to see the harbour and foreshore, the bridge, and Opera House.

Opera House ★★★

Beyond the Quay lies the Sydney Opera House, the city's most exciting and distinctive building. Australian writer and feminist Germaine Greer described it as 'bad taste', and others have echoed her sentiments. But the person who expressed the view of most Sydneysiders was John Douglas Pringle, an editor of the *Sydney Morning Herald*, who eloquently sang its praises, claiming it to be 'a building of which all Australians may rightly be proud, perhaps the only true work of architecture on this continent.'

The design for the Opera House was determined by an international competition announced in 1955. There were more than 230 entries from 32 countries. The £5000 was awarded to 38-year-old Danish architect, **Joern Utzon**.

Construction took 14 years and cost over $100 million, and there were constant battles between the architect and the NSW government, and compromises had to be made – the most significant being the reduction in size of the opera theatre. The project was funded by a state lottery.

The Sydney Opera House's famous 'wings' or 'shells' required extraordinary engineering skills. Three huge cranes were imported to Sydney from France to help install 2194 precast concrete ribs. The ribs were held

---

UNUSUAL FACTS ABOUT THE OPERA HOUSE

• The first public performance by a famous singer at the Opera House occurred long before the building was completed, when the African American singer Paul Robeson gave an impromptu concert for the workers.

• John Coburn's 'Curtain of the Sun', the curtain of the Opera House, was woven in Selletin, a village in France.

• In 1974 Dame Joan Sutherland, Australia's most famous post-war diva, sang all three soprano roles in the Australian Opera Company's production of Offenbach's *The Tales of Hoffman*.

• The roof of the Opera House is covered by 1,056,000 tiles and weighs 157,800 tons.

• Joern Utzon developed the idea of the roof shells by cutting segments from a sphere.

together by epoxy resin and 300km (186 miles) of tensioned cable. All this was covered by over 4000 lids which were surfaced by ceramic tiles made in Sweden.

People often think of the Sydney Opera House as just a single opera theatre. In fact, it has a five theatres – a concert hall, an opera theatre, a drama theatre, a cinema and a recording hall – as well two restaurants, a number of bars, six lounges, a library, five rehearsal studios and 65 dressing rooms.

The best way to arrive at the Opera House is to walk around Circular Quay from The Rocks. As you walk, you experience changing views of both Sydney Cove and the Opera House. There is the tang of the harbour in the air and you experience the true glory of the building. From the forecourts there are excellent views of the Quay and the Harbour Bridge. A number of restaurants, bars and cafés offer an ideal opportunity to pause and appreciate the beauty of this remarkable building.

There are regular **Guided Tours** of the building conducted daily (09:00–16:00) and **Backstage Tours** can also be arranged (Sun, 09:00–16:00). For more information, contact General Information on tel: (02) 9250-7111.

Opposite: *The hub of Sydney is Circular Quay, and it is here that the city's highlights – the ferries, Opera House, Harbour Bridge and a wall of city high-rise buildings – meet.*
Below: *The Opera House rivals the Harbour Bridge as the city's premier architectural icon. Its distinctive sail-like roof shells look splendid from any angle.*

Royal Botanic Gardens ★★

Beyond Circular Quay and the Opera House are Sydney's Royal Botanic Gardens, a beautiful retreat in the heart of the city. The magnificent gardens were first sown with seeds collected by Governor Phillip in Rio and Cape Town. In 1788 he proclaimed it farmland and named it Farm Cove. It became a Botanic Garden in 1816 when Governor Macquarie built a road to **Mrs Macquarie's Chair** and appointed Charles Fraser as superintendent.

Over the years the 29ha (70 acres) have been laid out so that there is now an Upper, Middle and Lower Garden through which nearly 2.5 million visitors stroll each year.

The Gardens, and the nearby **Domain**, are popular retreats for city workers who enjoy lunchtime picnics on the lawns or jog along the paths – an oasis in a busy city.

The Gardens have over 4000 trees and plants from all over the world. There are specialist collections in the herbarium and the pyramid glasshouse which supports a variety of tropical and sub-tropical plants.

The location of the gardens is ideal. A visitor who has spent the morning wandering through the Rocks, along the Quay and around the Opera House will find the tranquillity of the gardens a restorative before walking to Mrs Macquarie's Chair, the Art Gallery and the historic buildings of Macquarie Street.

Below: *There are over one million plant species in the arc and pyramid glasshouses of the Sydney Botanic Gardens.*

The gardens have a **Visitors Centre**, Gardens Shop and Gardens Restaurant and there are free guided walks which leave from the Centre (10:00 Wed and Fri; 13:00 Sun). The gardens are open from 6:30 to sunset. For information contact the Visitors Centre, tel: (02) 9231-8111 or (02) 9231-8125.

Mrs Macquarie's Chair **

To the east of the Opera House and the Gardens is **Mrs Macquarie's Chair** (or Lady Macquarie's Chair) from where Macquarie's wife enjoyed the harbour view. It remains one of the most popular of the harbour vantage points. In the late afternoon the Opera House and Harbour Bridge can be seen silhouetted against the setting sun.

Above: *The Art Gallery of New South Wales houses the state's collection ranging from early watercolours of the colony in Sydney Cove to major works by Australia's most important contemporary artists.*

Art Gallery and the Domain *

South of Mrs Macquarie's Chair is the Art Gallery of New South Wales and the Domain. Since the 19th century, the **Domain** has been a popular place for Sydneysiders, with speakers gathering on Sundays (much as they do at 'Speakers Corner' in London's Hyde Park) to put their viewpoints across to crowds of amused listeners. The Domain hosts a number of open-air concerts, like 'Carols by Candlelight', which are popular and attract massive crowds.

The **Art Gallery of New South Wales** houses a range of artworks from a substantial Aboriginal collection to modern Australian masters and excellent examples of the country's finest colonial artists. Of particular interest are the works of Conrad Martens (Australia's answer to J.M.W. Turner) and the huge, sensuous works of contemporary artists Lloyd Rees and Brett Whiteley. The gallery also contains works by European masters such as Picasso and Rembrandt.

The art gallery often has visiting exhibitions. Admission to the gallery is free, though it is common to pay for entry to the visiting exhibitions (open 10:00–17:00 daily). There are eating facilities and an excellent bookshop. For more information tel: (02) 9225-1744 or (02) 9225-1790.

MACQUARIE

The most innovative of all the early colonial governors, Lachlan Macquarie was born in 1761 on Ulva in the Scottish Hebrides. He arrived in 1810 with his wife, Elizabeth, and a black servant they had bought in India for 85 rupees. Macquarie was a visionary. During his governorship the Bank of New South Wales was established, the Blue Mountains were crossed, roads were built and over 200 towns were laid out.

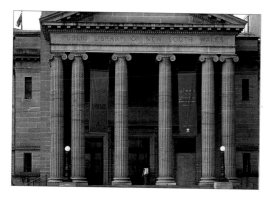

Above: *The most important library in NSW is located in Macquarie Street and was built around the remarkable collection of the bibliophile David Mitchell, who collected the finest Australiana during the latter 19th century.*

MACQUARIE STREET

Although Pitt Street and George Street are probably the 'main' streets of Sydney, Macquarie Street must be the city's most interesting. Once home to Sydney's high society, it runs from the **Opera House** to **Hyde Park** and is edged by the **Royal Botanic Gardens**, the **Conservatorium of Music**, the parliamentary complex and other historic buildings. There are handsome 19th-century townshouses and Georgian buildings, including the impressive **Royal Australian College of Surgeons**.

At the southern end is **Sydney Hospital**, built in 1880, and the NSW parliament. Nearby is **Martin Place**, centre of the banking district and containing the city's cenotaph and huge **General Post Office** building.

Mitchell Library ★

Known to Sydneysiders as the Mitchell Library, the **State Library of New South Wales** is the state's major repository of historic documents, sketches and information. The centrepiece of this interesting combination of old and new buildings is the Mitchell Library, the largest collection of colonial Australiana in the world. The core of the collection – the initial 61,000 volumes – was donated by David Scott Mitchell, an avid bibliophile who was one of the first 24 students at Sydney University (he graduated in 1859). The library has a number of regular events, including book readings (each year on 'Bloomsday', 16 June, James Joyce's *Ulysses* is read) and literary discussions, as well as a number of interesting exhibitions.

The reference library (09:00–17:00 Mon–Fri and 11:00–17:00 Sat and Sun) has regular film screenings and extensive data bases on most Australian topics. Entrance is free. For further information, tel: (02) 9230-1414.

MACQUARIE STREET IN THE 1920s

D.H. Lawrence's 1923 novel *Kangaroo* opens with the description: 'A bunch of work-men were lying on the grass of the park beside Macquarie Street, in the dinner hour. It was winter, the end of May, but the sun was warm, and they lay there in short sleeves, talking. Some were eating food from paper packages . . . Squatting and lying on the grassy bank beside the broad tarred road where taxis and hansom cabs passed continu-ally, they had that air of own-ing the city which belongs to a good Australian.'

Parliament House *

Built in 1810, **Parliament House** is one of the city's most elegant historic buildings. The Legislative Assembly is known to Sydneysiders as 'the bearpit' because of the no-holds-barred approach to debate (open Monday–Friday 09:00–12:00, 14:00–16:00). Guided tours are available when parliament isn't sitting. When parliament is in session it is possible to visit the Public Gallery and watch the state politicians 'debating' legislation. For more information, tel: (02) 9230-2111.

Sydney Mint Museum **

The Museum (open 10:00–17:00 daily) is located on the site of Australia's first mint and offers exhibitions based on Australia's history of gold mining and minting. There is an exhibition of the 2500-year history of gold coins, a history of gold discovery in Australia, and a display of gold and silver objects. Gold jewellery, coins, bullion, souvenirs can be bought from the Mint Gold Shop and souvenir medallions can be made.

Hyde Park Barracks ***

The Hyde Park Barracks next door were built in 1819 and now houses the Museum of Social History, which focuses on the lives of early convicts. An evocative soundscape designed to recreate convict life is a highlight.

HISTORY OF THE HYDE PARK BARRACKS

Now a tourist attraction the Hyde Park Barracks have an interesting history. They were built between 1817 and 1819 by convicts to house the colony's 800 convicts who, until that time, had been sleeping rough around Sydney. In the 1850s the building became a home for single immigrant women, then a home for destitute women. For many years it was used as an office block by the state government. In 1984 it was restored and opened as the Museum of Social History in New South Wales. It is now one of the city's most important reminders of its convict past.

Left: *At the southern end of Macquarie Street, the Sydney Mint Museum offers a range of exhibitions chronicling Australia's gold discoveries and the evolution of the country's currency.*

HYDE PARK AND SURROUNDS
Hyde Park ★

Hyde Park is a popular place for office workers seeking sunshine, trees and grassy lawns. Spread over 16ha (40 acres) it is divided by Park Street with the dominant feature of the southern section being the NSW **War Memorial** and the dominant feature in the northern section being the **Archibald Fountain**.

Hyde Park's gardens are formally laid out but the use of the park often hides this particular appeal. The lawns are worn down by pedestrians but flower beds nestle under the trees.

The War Memorial stands 30m (100ft) above the **Pool of Remembrance**. There is a Hall of Memory and a Hall of Silence. The Memorial is open daily. There is an exhibition of photographs of *Australians at War* in the basement. On Thursday at 13.00 the Australian Army forms a Guard of Honour outside.

St Andrew's Anglican Church ★

The foundation stone for what is Australia's oldest cathedral was laid in 1819 and the plans for a Gothic cathedral were drawn up by convict architect, Francis Greenway. There was a shortage of funds and it was redesigned by Edmund Blacket in 1837. It was eventually consecrated on 30 November 1868 – St Andrew's Day.

St Mary's Roman Catholic Cathedral *

Built on the site of the original Church of the Blessed Virgin Mary (1821), the Gothic-style St Mary's Cathedral, to the east of Hyde Park, is still incomplete (the twin spires were never added) although the foundation stone was laid in 1868. Today it is the centre of Sydney's large Roman Catholic community.

Above: *St Mary's Roman Catholic Cathedral, with its distinctive main spires, lies opposite tranquil Hyde Park.*

THE CENTRAL BUSINESS DISTRICT

Sydney's CBD is a mixture of office blocks and specialist shops ranging from department stores (such as David Jones and Grace Bros) to *haute couture*. Of interest are art galleries and gift shops including the **Heart of Australia Gallery** at 77 Castlereagh Street which sells didgeridoos, Aboriginal dot paintings from the Western desert and handcarved artefacts (tel: (02) 9223-7595); **New Guinea Primitive Arts**, Queen Victoria Building, offering a range of tribal artefacts (tel: (02) 9267-5134); **Goodwood Saddlery and Outback Store**, 237 Broadway, selling distinctively Australian clothes such as Akubra hats, R.M. Williams boots and Drizabone coats (tel: (02) 9660-6788); **Australian Wine Centre**, Goldfields House at Circular Quay, with over 1000 Australian wines (tel: (02) 9247-2755); and **Strand Hatters**, Strand Arcade, 412 George Street, has a comprehensive collection of Australian hats which are popular with visitors wanting to protect themselves from the harsh sunshine (tel: (02) 9231-6884).

Sydney's day-to-day shopping has tended to move more towards suburban shopping malls and the city has had to concentrate on specialist shops designed to cater for visitors. While it is not the Australian custom to bargain (you are expected to pay the marked price), shop around to get the best price for a particular item. Shop rentals are high so you will find price variations.

EATING IN THE CBD

There are a number of excellent restaurants in the city centre which have become popular with visitors to the city. Here are three of the best.

• **Daniel's Steakhouse**, 1 Bent St, tel: (02) 9251-6977. Rated by its regular patrons as the best steakhouse in the city.

• **Bilsons**, Circular Quay West, tel: (02) 9251-5600. Rated by most of the city's food experts as one of the ten best restaurants in the state.

• **Edna's Table**, Martin Place, tel: (02) 9231-1400. An opportunity to eat genuine Aussie *haute cuisine* – try the kangaroo steaks, smoked emu, kangaroo pâté and Tasmanian oysters.

Queen Victoria Building ★★
Described by couturier Pierre Cardin as 'the most beautiful shopping centre in the world', the 'QVB' was built in 1898 to resemble a Byzantine palace. Much neglected, it was restored at a cost of $75 million and re-opened in 1982. It is a centre of high fashion, but also has a fast food takeaway area and many high-turnover gift shops. For general information, tel: (02) 9264-9209.

Above: *While Sydney's dominant architecture is the modern high-rise, many 19th-century buildings have been preserved. Both the QVB (pictured here) and the Strand Arcade are fine examples of old-world elegance.*

ATTRACTIONS AT THE QVB

The **Queen Victoria Building** is a shopping mall and a tourist attraction. Make sure you see:
• The **wishing well** at the southern end of the building with a bronze statue of Queen Victoria's favourite dog, 'Islay'.
• Paintings featuring the life of **Queen Victoria** (Top Level).
• The **Royal Clock** which chimes on the hour from 09:00–21:00 (Top Level).
• Reproductions of the **Crown Jewels** (Top Level).
• Restored leadlight windows and winding metal stairways.
• The **crystal dome**, hand-crafted from cathedral glass.

Centrepoint Tower ★★
Views from the Observation Deck are remarkable and give the visitor an understanding of the layout of the city: to the north across Sydney Harbour, to the west across to the Blue Mountains, to the south across Botany Bay and Sydney Airport towards the Royal National Park, and east to the Harbour Heads and the Pacific Ocean. Located at 100 Market Street it is open every day and night. For more information, tel: (02) 9229-7444. Those who want to eat while they enjoy the view should make a booking at the **Sydney Tower Restaurant** (tel: (02) 9233-3722) located on two levels: one for à la carte, the other a buffet-style menu.

Duty Free Shopping
Australia is very cheap by international standards (five-star hotels are about half the cost of European equivalents), and there are many duty free stores near the international airports and in the CBD. There are a number of specialist duty free shops in the city centre. If you have an airline or sea cruise ticket out of Australia, most well-established stores can provide you with goods at duty free rates. The only obligation is that you must not open or use the goods before you pass through Customs at your port of departure. The saving, which is simply the removal of local sales tax, varies from 10 to 25% depending on the item.

MUSEUMS

Australian Museum **

The museum, at 6 College Street near Hyde Park, is the nation's oldest and largest natural history museum. Its displays of Australian flora and fauna are considered the country's finest. The repository has over 8 million pieces, and some experts rate it as one of the world's top natural history museums. There are exhibitions on Aboriginal culture, Australian wildlife and dinosaurs. Features also include exhibitions on Australia's ecology ('Dreamtime to Dust') and a hands-on exhibit ('Discovery Space').

The museum, which has its own restaurant and a shop which sells Australian artefacts and natural history books, is open daily (09:30–17:00). For details of current exhibitions, contact the Museum's Alive Line, tel: 0055 29408.

Powerhouse Museum **

This outstanding science, arts and technology museum located behind Darling Harbour, boasts exhibits ranging from the state's first steam train to the huge Boulton and Watt steam engine (1780). The museum also includes exhibitions of furniture, clothing and aeroplanes, and it has special areas for children, regular specialist exhibitions and a restaurant decorated by the popular Australian artist Ken Done.

Displays include historical costumes, a Wedgwood collection and fine Thomas Hope furniture. The very popular space technology display combines pieces from the USA, USSR and Chinese space programs.

Daily events include an hourly demonstration of the elaborate 'Strasburg' clock. Over 100 exhibits are interactive. Two to four hours are needed to enjoy a cross-section of exhibits.

CITY MUSEUMS

- **Australian Museum**, 6 College St, East Sydney, tel: (02) 9320-6000 (09:30–17:00 daily, half price Saturday).
- **Australian National Maritime Museum**, Pyrmont Bridge, Darling Harbour, tel: (02) 9552-7500 (10:00–17:00 daily).
- **Hyde Park Barracks Museum**, Queens Square, Macquarie St, tel: (02) 9223-8922 (10:00–17:00 daily).
- **Powerhouse Museum**, 500 Harris St, Ultimo, tel: (02) 9217-0111 (10:00–17:00 daily).
- **Sydney Mint Museum**, Macquarie St, tel: (02) 9217-0311. (10:00–17:00 daily)
- **Sydney Observatory**, Watson Road, The Rocks tel: (02) 9217-0485. (10:00–17:00 and, for night viewings,18:15–20:15 daily).

Below: *The Powerhouse Museum, on the edge of Darling Harbour.*

JAPANESE RESTAURANTS

In recent years Sydney's Japanese restaurants have become increasingly popular.
- **Fuuki**, 417 Pacific Hwy, Crows Nest, tel: (02) 436-1608. Friendly, family-style Japanese restaurant.
- **Isaribi**, 41 Elizabeth Bay Rd, Elizabeth Bay, tel: (02) 358-2125. A wonderful Japanese grill room.
- **Suntory**, 529 Kent St, tel: (02) 267-2900. Considered the best Japanese restaurant in Sydney.
- **Kamogawa**, 177 Sussex St, tel: (02) 299-5533. Kaiseki-style cooking offering one delicious course after another.
- **Yutaka**, 200 Crown St, East Sydney, tel: (02) 361-3818. Famous for sushi and sashimi.

Australian National Maritime Museum ★★

At the northern end of Darling Harbour, the Australian National Maritime Museum is designed as an overview of the island continent's relationship with the sea. It centres around six themes: the continent's discovery, the long sea voyages involved, the commercial value of the sea, the sea and leisure, the Australian Navy (it is possible to board a Navy destroyer), and the links between Australia and the USA across the Pacific. There are also a number of changing exhibitions. Contact tel: (02) 9552-7500 or the Infoline on tel: 0055 62002 (open 10:00–17:00 daily).

Museum of Contemporary Art ★★

The MCA, in the old art deco Maritime Services Board Building on the western side of Circular Quay, offers a cross-section of international contemporary art. Masterpieces include Roy Lichtenstein's *Crying Girl* and Robert Indiana's *Love*. It is one of the city's cultural centres being used for lectures, films and concerts.

One of the top attractions is the restaurant which not only serves excellent, reasonably priced meals, but allows the diner to sit and watch people walking towards The Rocks and ferries coming and going at Circular Quay. The restaurant (open 11:00–18:00 daily) is an ideal meeting place. For more information contact tel: (02) 9252-4033.

Below: *The Museum of Contemporary Art near the Circular Quay.*

DARLING HARBOUR ★★

Darling Harbour is the city's equivalent to San Francisco's Fisherman's Wharf – a large complex of hotels, museums, shops, restaurants, fast food eateries and a parade of entertainment all set against a backdrop of the harbour.

Before 1988, the harbour was a rundown collection of wharves and warehouses. It has been converted into one Sydney's premier attractions.

Left: *Once part of the city's bustling waterfront, Darling Harbour has been converted into an area with conference centres, four-star accommodation, quality restaurants and excellent shopping facilities.*

Getting Around Darling Harbour

Built amid much controversy, the **monorail** runs from Darling Harbour (which has four stops) to the city centre. It is a cheap and efficient way to visit the harbour. For more than two trips, buy a Monorail Day Pass.

At the northern end of Darling Harbour, near the aquarium, a **ferry service** runs every 30 minutes. It completes a circuit stopping at Balmain, McMahons Point and Circular Quay. It is a pleasant short journey around to The Rocks and the Opera House.

Stop at the **Visitors Centre** for maps, daily information and information about special 'deals', (09:00–17:00, daily). For details, tel: (02) 9286-0111.

Entertainment

Sydney is famed for its excellent seafood restaurants, and **Jordan's** at Darling Harbour has a pleasant outdoor setting where a wide range of seafood can be eaten while enjoying the view across the boats moored in the harbour. If you don't want to spend time in a restaurant there are a number of fast food places in the food hall of the shopping complex.

The Darling Harbour complex prides itself on its free entertainment. Most weekends, and often during the week, musicians will be performing at Tumbalong Park or on the shores of Cockle Bay.

DARLING HARBOUR SUPER TICKET

Travellers looking for a sensible bargain should purchase a Darling Harbour Super Ticket. Valid for three months and modestly priced, the ticket provides entry to the **Chinese Garden**, the **Aquarium**, offers trips on the Matilda **See Sydney Cruise** (either a 90min or 2hr journey) and the **monorail**, provides a 10% discount voucher to over 200 stores in the **Darling Harbour Shopping Complex**, and supplies a meal either at the **Craig Brewery Bar & Bistro** at the southern end of Darling Harbour or a barbeque on the Matilda See Sydney Cruise. It is a significant saving on regular prices and offers a comprehensive overview of Darling Harbour's main attractions.

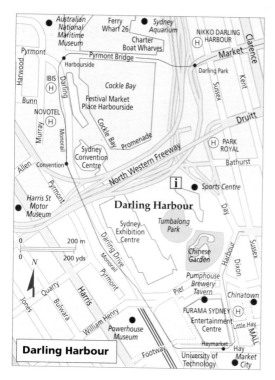

Darling Harbour

Sydney Aquarium ***

The aquarium boasts an outstanding collection of exhibits which provide a comprehensive overview of Australian aquatic life – from seals and crocodiles to sharks, stingrays and the wide range of fish which live in Sydney Harbour. There is also a pool where visitors can touch the crustaceans and molluscs that live on the shoreline (09:30 –21:00 daily). For details, tel: (02) 9262-2300.

Darling Harbour has many excellent hotels including the Hotel Nikko, the Novotel, the Parkroyal, the Ibis and the Furama. All are central, with easy access to the city centre by monorail, walking or taxi.

CHINATOWN **

Lying to the southeast of Darling Harbour is Sydney's colourful Chinatown. The Chinese first settled in Australia during the gold rushes of the 1850s. Although they were subjected to considerable racial prejudice on the goldfields, the small number who stayed did not congregate in ghettoes but rather dispersed themselves throughout the rural areas of Australia. The census of 1871 revealed that 54 towns and 75 rural districts had Chinese populations of up to 10 people.

Today Chinatown is a popular centre for Australian Chinese and for more recent immigrants and students from Southeast Asia. In the past decade large numbers of Asians, many of them refugees from Indo-China, have arrived to pursue a new life.

Dixon Street **

Chinatown, which centres around **Dixon Street**, is a showpiece for Chinese and Asian culture in Australia and offers the visitor a range of outstanding restaurants which include cuisines from Vietnam and Thailand as well as regional varieties of Chinese cooking. The restaurants in the area range from small takeaway places in a number of large food halls to expensive *haute cuisine* locations which include dancing and floor shows. Each visit to Chinatown is an adventure. Most Sydneysiders have their favourite restaurants, but these are based more often on familiarity than a sense of the superiority of the cuisine.

The Chinese Gardens **

Situated at the northern end of Chinatown and at the southern end of the Darling Harbour complex, the gardens are a symbol of Chinese involvement in Australian life. This traditional Chinese garden, reputedly the largest of its type outside China, is based on gardening principles which date back to the 5th century. It is designed as a place of peacefulness and tranquillity, with miniature mountains, lakes, waterfalls, forests and flowers. It has been constructed so that each vantage point offers an image of China in miniature, (09:30–sunset, daily).

> **CHINATOWN RESTAURANTS**
>
> There are too many restaurants in Chinatown to do them all justice. Here are some of the more famous ones.
> • **Marigold**, 299 Sussex St, tel: (02) 9264-6744. Cantonese-style cooking. Famous for its yum cha.
> • **Regal**, 347–353 Sussex St, tel: (02) 9261-8988. Favourite Cantonese restaurant that has served the Sydney community for years.
> • **Superbowl Peking**, 494 Sussex St, tel: (02) 9211-1568. The best of the Hong Kong kitchens in Sydney.
> • **Jing May**, Level 1, Prince Centre, 8 Quay St, tel: 9281-2387. The perfect noodle restaurant that delights the tastebuds and the wallet.

Left: *The Chinese Gardens are located at the southern end of Darling Harbour and the northern end of Chinatown. A peaceful respite from the bustling city that surrounds them, they have been designed on gardening principles which date back to the 5th century. There are miniature mountains, lakes, waterfalls, forests and flowers.*

3
Exploring the Inner City

Like most major cities, Sydney can be divided between those who live in the inner city and those who live in suburbia. The inner city people enjoy the close proximity of the city centre, being only five or ten minutes away from good restaurants, cinemas, theatres, concert venues and nightclubs. In Sydney these people typically live in flats, apartments or terrace houses – often old working class accommodation which has been modernised – with little or no garden and neighbours only a wall away. While only a few people live in the central business district this is more than compensated by the dense populations of Kings Cross, Potts Point, Elizabeth Bay, Paddington, Surry Hills, Darlinghurst, Glebe, Newtown, Rozelle and Balmain.

KINGS CROSS *

The most famous, or 'infamous', of all the inner city areas is Kings Cross – Sydney's equivalent to London's Soho. In the 1930s Kings Cross was the centre of the city's bohemian community. This continued up to the 1960s when 'the Cross', as it is known, was still a strange and wonderful mixture of high-class hotels, bohemians, prostitutes, strip clubs, nightclubs and quality restaurants.

Most Sydneysiders feel that the demise of the Cross can be dated to the arrival of the American servicemen on leave from Vietnam in the mid-1960s. They injected huge amounts of cash into the economy and this inevitably changed the area's 'charm' into something more malevolent and overtly commercial.

DON'T MISS

*** Paddo Bazaar: 395 Oxford Street, Paddington, one of Sydney's best street markets. Open Saturday.
** Oxford Street: experience the ambience of the city's most fashionable late-night street.
** Gleebooks: 191 Glebe Point Rd, Glebe, voted the best bookshop in Australia in 1995.
* Macleay Street, Kings Cross: nights are colourful and bursting with life.
* Queen Street, Woollahra: stylish and elegant.

Opposite: *Sydney's inner suburbs are the city's pulse with people preferring to live here rather than in the city.*

Today the Cross is still a tourist attraction with many excellent hotels and fine restaurants. However, it has acquired a reputation as a centre of hardcore pornography, drugs and crime. If Sydney has a violent heartland (and, as a general principle, it is still safe to walk most of the city's streets at night with confidence) then the Cross is it. The only advice to the visitor is 'Be careful'.

Having offered that warning, what are the attractions of Kings Cross? It is important to remember that Kings Cross is truly schizophrenic. It is Dr Jekyll by day and Mr Hyde by night. In the daytime the leafy parks and tree-lined streets, the smell of coffee from the

EATING AT KINGS CROSS

Kings Cross is known for its excellent restaurants. Here are some of the well-known ones.
• **Bayswater Brasserie**, 32 Bayswater Rd, tel: (02) 9357-2177. Much-loved brasserie in the heart of Kings Cross.
• **Darley Street Thai**, 28–30 Bayswater Rd, tel: (02) 9358-6530. Thai cooking at its very best.
• **Mesclun**, 33 Bayswater Rd, tel: (02) 9358-5582. Fresh ingredients and imaginative preparation make this restaurant an experience.
• **Mezzaluna**, 123 Victoria St, tel: (02) 9357-1988. Outstanding *nouveau* Italian-style cuisine.
• **Pond**, 62–64 Kellet St, tel: (02) 9368-0555. Award-winning restaurant that prides itself on unusual taste thrills.

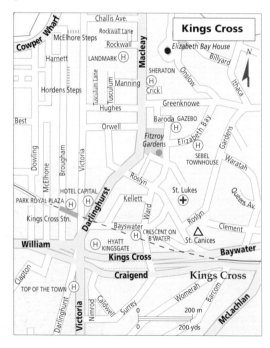

numerous excellent cafés and eateries and the attractive-ness of the **El Alamein fountain** are all magnets. Victoria Street to the south of the Kings Cross tunnel has some outstanding places to eat and its cafés offer some of the best coffee in Sydney.

Perhaps the greatest attraction is just sitting in a café and watching the world go by. Watching the *demi monde* emerge around lunchtime, with their dark glasses and world-weary demeanour, is fascinating.

The area is a major accommodation location offering numerous cheap backpacker hostels. This has meant that many of the shops are geared to tourism, offering Australiana and gifts.

OXFORD STREET **

Oxford Street is what Kings Cross used to be. It is the heart of Sydney's nightlife. A wonderful strip of hotels, nightclubs, restaurants, late-night bookshops, cinemas and cafés, Oxford Street is where those people who have no trouble partying until dawn gather, prome-nade and generally enjoy themselves.

Historically the street has long been associated with the city's large gay community. A decade ago it was an almost exclusively gay domain, with hotels like the **Exchange** and the **Albury** being well-known gay hang-outs. There were numerous darkened bars with mirror balls and loud disco/dance music, and the streets were alive with men fresh from the gym flashing their gleaming muscles and parading their neat moustaches and haircuts up and down the strip. Slowly the bars, because of their atmosphere and loud music, began to reach beyond their original gay con-stituency. This was combined with the slow decline of Kings Cross. Today Oxford Street is a major centre for those seeking a little excitement.

Opposite: *Kings Cross lies to the east of Sydney's central business district. Historically it stood at the top of the William Street hill until a tunnel to the eastern suburbs forced this vibrant centre to shift north into Macleay Street and Darlinghurst Road.*
Below: *Kings Cross is famous as the centre of Sydney's nightlife: a potent mixture of nightclubs, bars, fast-food outlets, upmarket restaurants and hotels.*

Oxford Street, as a nightspot, extends from the south-eastern corner of Hyde Park up to Taylor Square (this is the main 'drag') and beyond to Victoria Barracks and through Paddington to Five Ways. Between Hyde Park and Taylor Square the street is a constant tapestry of excitement. There are numerous pubs and restaurants, a number of upstairs bars and clubs, and, if you look carefully, some very good restaurants.

Kinselas at Taylor Square is one of the city's well-known nightspots with entertainment ranging from international acts to lesbian nights. The ground floor, where free live music is performed most nights of the week, is decorated like a typical Australian bar. The middle floor is a quieter cocktail lounge, and the upstairs, which was once an undertaker's embalming room, is decorated like an old-style cabaret venue.

Beyond Taylor Square is Oxford Street's restaurant centre. The Balkan restaurants have been here since the 1960s; the Indian, Thai and Italian restaurants are more recent additions.

Further down the street the **Academy Twin** and the **Verona**, two of the city's finest art cinemas, regularly show foreign language films. Over the road the **Ariel Bookshop** is open late every evening. It is one of the city's best bookshops and is a popular place for book launches. **Berkelouw Books** is opposite and has an extensive range of secondhand books and an upstairs café.

Further up the hill, Oxford Street passes the Royal Women's Hospital and **Paddington Town Hall** (home to the excellent **Chauvel Cinema**) and moves into another strip of coffee shops, restaurants, bars and bookshops. The **New Edition Bookshop** is worth visiting, as is **Juniper Hall**, located opposite the Town Hall.

Oxford Street is, in fact, fun both day and night.

PADDINGTON **

Located 3km (2 miles) southeast of the city centre, Paddington is arguably Sydney's most self-consciously chic and arty suburb. Once a predominantly working-class inner city suburb, it was gentrified in the 1960s and is now an expensive and popular centre for city professionals and those who would consider themselves 'arty' – art entrepreneurs, journalists, advertising people, public relations experts and their ilk.

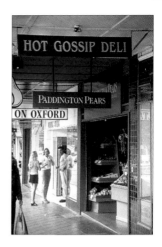

This gentrification was greatly helped by the suburb's proximity to the unambiguously wealthy suburbs of Double Bay, Woollahra and Point Piper and the fact that a number of the streets – particularly **Queen Street** and **Jersey Road** – had some of the city's finest 19th-century terrace houses.

The appeal of Paddington lies in its bookshops, art galleries, restaurants, cafés and pubs. The best way to see the suburb is to simply wander. Start at Paddington Town Hall and walk up Oxford Street, browse in the record and bookshops, have a cup of tea or coffee at the **New Edition Tea Rooms** (next door to the **New Edition Bookshop**), then wander down the sidestreets where specialist chocolate shops, antique dealers, restaurants and art galleries are scattered among beautifully restored terrace houses. The suburb is basically a journey of discovery. Unlike most Australian suburbs it does not have a standard grid street pattern. The streets head off at strange angles from each other and wind around the side of the slopes which fall towards the harbour. There is still a sense of adventure in this charming suburb.

Above: *In Paddington, Oxford Street is a classic example of Sydney's inner city ribbon development, with fruit and vegetable shops catering for local shoppers next to chic bookshops, cafés and bars.*
Opposite: *Oxford Street in Darlinghurst is the centre of Sydney's gay community. At night the street is alive with bars, dance venues, clubs and shops specialising in gay attire. During the day it is a subdued thoroughfare with shopfronts hinting at its nocturnal activities.*

Victoria Barracks **

Paddington came into existence in the late 1840s–early 1850s when simple accommodation for soldiers was built after the construction of **Victoria Barracks**. Between 1860 and 1890 nearly 4000 houses for working people were built near the Barracks and, inevitably, shopkeepers and publicans moved in to meet the needs of the local community.

Above: *The streets behind Paddington's main thoroughfares boast some of Sydney's most beautiful 19th-century terrace houses.*

Juniper Hall *

The oldest house in the suburb is **Juniper Hall** on Oxford Street, opposite the **Paddington Town Hall**. It was built in 1822 and named after the berries which produced gin at the brewery down the hill. The name was later changed to Ormond House to remove the 'boozy' associations and, in the 1980s, the building – and its original name – was restored by the National Trust. It is now a private business, although people curious about the building often walk in and take photographs.

Paddington Markets **

A popular weekend haunt is the 'Paddo' Bazaar at 395 Oxford Street, (Sat 10:00–16:00). On offer are crafts, foods and handmade garments. Its location on Oxford Street ensures that the market's patrons are a typical cross-section of inner-city residents and tourists. The Paddington Market has been operating since the mid-1970s and has slowly evolved into one of Sydney's tourist attractions.

Galleries **

Paddington has become Sydney's commercial gallery centre. There are nearly 30 galleries – all selling a range of original artworks by some of Australia's most talented artists – located in the suburb. The most famous include the **Australian Galleries** (tel: (02) 9360-5177) which specializes in contemporary Australian artworks including paintings, art books and limited edition prints; the **Barry Stern Galleries** (tel: (02) 9331-4676) which, apart from selling a wide range of Australian art, also holds regular exhibitions; the **Christopher Day Gallery** (tel: (02) 9326-1952) which has changing exhibitions of traditional and modern Australian painting; **Coo-ee Aboriginal Art**

RED AND BLUE BUS PASSES

The best way to explore central Sydney and the Eastern Suburbs is to buy Red and Blue Bus passes. The 'Red' **Sydney Explorer** buses cover a 35km (22 miles) circuit which includes 26 stops at historical sites and harbour vantage points. The journey runs from the city centre to the area around Kings Cross, across to Darling Harbour and over the Harbour Bridge to North Sydney. Contact tel: 13 1500. The 'Blue' **Bondi & Bay Explorer** has 20 stops. It runs from the city centre along the Eastern Suburbs to Watsons Bay, turns south through Bondi to Coogee, and returns to the city via Randwick and Centennial Park; tel: 13 1500.

(tel: (02) 9332-1544) which has a large range of Aboriginal gifts, fabrics, books and posters, as well as paintings, sculpture and limited edition prints by traditional and urban artists; the **Hogarth Galleries/Aboriginal Art Centre** (tel: (02) 9360-6839) has a huge collection of traditional and urban Aboriginal art; the **Holdsworth Galleries** (tel: (02) 9363-1364); **Rex Irwin Art Dealer** (tel: (02) 9363-3212), a gallery dealing in important Australian and European contemporary art; **Roslyn Oxley Gallery** (tel: (02) 9331-1919), acknowledged as one of the city's finest galleries for contemporary art; the **Sherman Galleries** (tel: (02) 9360-5566) has a sculpture garden as well as important exhibitions of contemporary Australian and international art; and the **Watters Gallery** (tel: (02) 9331-2556) which is well known as one of the best exhibitors of contemporary Australian art.

Left: The Paddington markets have become one of Sydney's premier inner-city attractions. Offering a bewildering array of goods, the markets are located at the upper end of Oxford Street.
Below: Paddington is a suburb of art galleries and pubs. Down the hill from Oxford Street is the Five Ways, a small shopping centre and the excellent Royal Hotel.

A very handy free directory – titled *Paddington Galleries & Environs* is published annually by the Paddington Art Gallery (tel: (02) 9332-840).

Eating and Shopping

Paddington has an extensive range of restaurants, brasseries and cafés. The emphasis is on informal eating. While it is generally a good idea to pre-book, the eateries on Oxford Street are geared to passing trade. In fact, some of them are so informal they will not take bookings.

Below: *Oxford Street,
Paddington is a shopper's
delight, with shops specialising in everything from
sculptured cakes to secondhand and new clothing.*

If a restaurant is full, you will usually only have to wait 10–15 minutes for a table. There are many specialized Oxford Street restaurants which include vegetarian, Spanish, Thai and Indian food, all-day breakfasts, and there are plenty of bijou coffee lounges.

The upper end of Oxford Street is well known for reasonably priced clothes shops and high fashion boutiques.

NEWTOWN

In the past 30 years, 'fashion' has swept inner city suburbs. In the 1960s, Balmain and Paddington were 'gentrified'; they were followed by Glebe, Surry Hills, Darlinghurst and Rozelle. One of the most recent additions is Newtown. For years the suburb was a classic example of Sydney's 'ribbon development' – the peculiar situation where a suburb's entire shopping centre was only one shop deep and stretched for some distance along a main artery. It is also a characteristic of the suburbs of Leichhardt (Parramatta Road) and Paddington (Oxford Street).

King Street ★★

In the case of Newtown, the shopping facilities on either side of **King Street** were always the hub of the suburb. By the 1920s the street boasted 'a splendid tram service

every two or three minutes down King Street; fare 3d; also all night trams'. This description included the fact that the street was 'wood-blocked for one and three quarter miles in length lined on both sides with shops, one of the busiest suburban thoroughfares, and at the bridge is situated the station tramway depot'.

Left: *Sydney's most bohemian street of cafés, restaurants and interesting shops is King Street.*

Today King Street is a mixture of interesting pubs (including a few very popular gay bars), a bewildering array of restaurants and cafés ranging from Indonesian and Nepalese through to excellent Indian fast food outlets, African food, Italian pasta, Vietnamese and, in the case of the **Thai Pothong** and **Thai Land**, two of the city's best Thai restaurants.

The emphasis is on informality: people simply park behind King Street and wander past bookshops (visit **Gould's Bookshop** simply to experience the chaos that can result from too many books) and unusual gift shops, and decide on a restaurant or café on the basis of the smells or the chalkboard menu outside.

For those interested in history a walk down the side-streets off King Street will reveal the diversity of the suburb: small worker's terraces are cheek-to-cheek with handsome two- and three-storey terraces and, in some cases, very fine freestanding Victorian residences.

St Stephen's **

The historical heart of the suburb is the beautiful **St Stephen's Church of England** in Church Street (off King Street) which was built by one of Sydney's most admired architects, Edmund Blacket, who also designed the central quadrangle at Sydney University. Located in the church cemetery is the grave of Miss

---

EATING ON KING STREET

Sydney's newest eating place with lots of interesting surprises including:
- **Ban Thai**, 115–117 King St, tel: (02) 9519-5330. Thai cooking catering for the whole family.
- **Old Saigon**, 107 King St, tel: (02) 9519-5931. An interesting mix of Vietnamese and Thai makes this a popular restaurant.
- **The Fish Tank**, 119 King St, tel: (02) 9557-5627. Exceptional seafood.
- **Le Lavandou**, 143 King St, tel: (02) 9233-5237. Quality French cuisine served with Gallic charm.
- **Thai Pothong**, 294 King St, tel: (02) 9550-6277. Considered the best Thai cooking on King Street.
- **Three Five Seven King**, 357 King St, Contemporary bistro food served with flair.

Donnithorne, thought by many to be the model for Charles Dickens' famous character, Miss Havisham. Jilted by her lover on her wedding day, Miss Donnithorne became a recluse and really did leave her wedding breakfast undisturbed for decades.

Above: *Sydney University is the city's oldest tertiary institution. Located just west of the city centre, its quadrangle, designed by the architect Edmund Blacket, was modelled on the colleges of Oxford and Cambridge.*

Sydney University ★★

Apart from its central quadrangle, a very self-conscious colonial attempt to mimic the academic glory of Oxbridge, it has a number of interesting museums. The **Macleay Museum** specializes in zoology, photography and anthropology, and includes specimens collected by both Joseph Banks (who sailed up the coast with Cook) and Charles Darwin. (8:30–16:30 Tue–Fri, tel: (02) 9351-2274). The **Nicholson Museum of Antiquities** has an excellent collection of Greek and Egyptian artefacts (10:00–16:30 Mon–Fri, tel: (02) 9351-2812).

EATING ON GLEBE POINT ROAD

A street of a thousand tastes and cuisines. Here are some interesting restaurants worth trying.

• **Darling Mills**, 134 Glebe Point Rd, tel: (02) 9660-5666. Australian elegance in this beautifully renovated turn-of-the-century building.
• **Iku Wholefood Kitchen**, 25a Glebe Point Rd, tel: (02) 9692-8720. Vegetarian food with flair.
• **Flavour of India**, 142 Glebe Point Rd, tel: (02) 9692-0062. Corner restaurant with the authentic taste of India.
• **Tanjore**, 34 Glebe Point Rd, tel: (02) 9660-6332. Honest Indian food with a reasonable price tag.

GLEBE **

To the north of Sydney university is the suburb of Glebe. In 1789 it was originally set aside by Governor Arthur Phillip as church land. Most of it had been sold by 1828 and, over the next 50 years, gracious Victorian residences were built in the area. But the fortunes of these beautiful buildings have since changed. **Toxteth House**, considered by The Glebe Society as 'possibly the most important landmark in Glebe', changed from a private home to a boarding house. Toxteth House eventually became part of St Scholastica's School.

Lyndhurst **

This Regency villa located in Darghan Street was built for James Bowman, the principal surgeon at Sydney Hospital. It was completed around 1835, and has been used as a university, boarding house, hospital and meeting house for the Free Presbyterian Church. In the 1970s it was restored and it is now the headquarters of the NSW Historic Houses Trust.

Glebe Point Road **

If you want to explore the suburb's history, go to **Gleebooks** (open 8:00–21:00 daily) located at 191 Glebe Point Road (it is regarded as one of the best bookshops in Australia) and purchase a copy of The Glebe Society's guide *Historical Glebe*, which provides fascinating details about all of the suburb's most interesting buildings, including its many historic churches and rows of terrace houses.

Like Oxford Street in Paddington (*see* p. 47) and King Street in Newtown (*see* p. 52), **Glebe Point Road** is another example of inner city ribbon development. A row of shops stretches all the way along the road which offers a range of interesting restaurants and cafés, antique shops, bookshops and galleries. The popular **Valhalla Cinema** specializes in art movies, re-releases and features late-night cult movies, particularly on Friday and Saturday nights.

SUNDAY MARKETS

Sunday in Sydney is an ideal time to explore the city's many street markets.
• **Asian Noodle Market**, North Sydney, lunchtime; tel: (02) 9417-3256.
• **Bondi Beach Markets**, Bondi Beach, all day.
• **Kings Cross Market**, Kings Cross, 09:00–17:00; tel: (02) 9368-1961.
• **Manly Arts & Crafts Market**, Manly, 08:30–19:30
• **Opera House Forecourt Market**, Opera House, 11:00–18:00; tel: 018286 320.
• **Rozelle Market**, Darling St, Rozelle, 09:00–16:00; tel: (02) 9818-5373.
• **The Rocks Market**, George St, The Rocks, 10:00–18:00.

Opposite: *Once owned by the Church of England, the Sydney suburb of Glebe is now a bustling inner city residential and shopping centre.*

BALMAIN ★★★

Beyond Glebe lie the historic suburbs of **Balmain** and **Birchgrove**. Like Paddington, these are suburbs with strong working-class traditions which were gentrified in the 1960s. Today there are few remnants of the original residents. Some houses, particularly those with water views, sell for over $1 million and are the residences of wealthy actors, musicians, writers, artists, advertising executives and other professionals wanting to live close to the city.

The transformation of Balmain from a complex mixture of social groups to a prestigious suburb is almost complete. The main artery, **Darling Street**, is characterized by chic delicatessens, restaurants, galleries, bookshops and expensive specialist shops.

It is hard to imagine that this was once a predominantly industrial suburb. The excellent local guidebook *Around Balmain*, published by The Balmain Association, notes: 'In the 1850s Mort's Dock opened . . . it was followed by Booth's Steam Sawmill, the Austin Soap Works, the Union Box Company, Elliott Brothers Chemical Works and Hutchinson's Candle Factory'.

The best time to visit Balmain is on Saturday when an exploration of the suburb's interesting past can be combined with a visit to the **Balmain Market** (07:30–16:00; for details tel: (02) 810-3712). Be sure to travel to the eastern end of the suburb, where it slopes down to the harbour.

Below: *Sydney Harbour boasts 13 islands, each with a unique character.*

The Harbour Islands **

There are 13 islands on Sydney Harbour. Each has its own extraordinary history ranging from the tiny 5.5ha (14 acres) **Goat Island** which was used as a quarry for some of the city's early sandstone buildings, through to **Cockatoo Island** which, for most of this century, has been used as a dry dock. In the 1920s it was the largest dry dock in the world.

Access to the individual islands varies, with some – **Glebe Island** is now a container terminal and **Garden Island** is a naval base – restricted to the public. Some of the main islands are Goat, Shark, Cocatoo, Clarke and Fort Denison.

Fort Denison **

The most popular and accessible is **Fort Denison**, sometimes known as 'Pinchgut' or 'Rock Island'. The island was originally used as a place of punishment for difficult convicts. As early as 11 February 1788 a convict named Thomas Hill was sentenced to a week on bread and water in irons on 'the small white rocky Island adjacent to this Cove'. By 1796 a gibbet had been installed on the island,

---

SYDNEY HARBOUR'S ISLANDS

There are 13 islands in Sydney Harbour. Six are named after people, and of the others there is a Goat Island, Shark Island, Snapper Island and Cockatoo Island. Shark Island wasn't named as a result of the sharks in the harbour but rather because it has the shape of a shark. Clarke Island was named after Lieutenant Ralph Clarke who arrived in Sydney with the First Fleet and established a garden on the tiny island. The bushranger Captain Thunderbolt swam to freedom across the dangerous waters from Cockatoo Island to the harbour shore.

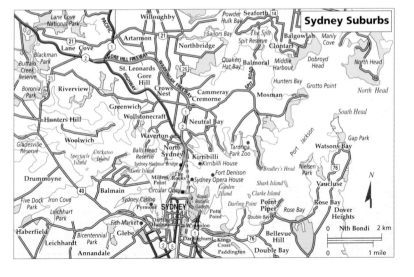

Sydney Suburbs

Above: *It is possible to travel from Birchgrove to the city centre by both bus and ferry.*

and convicts who were sentenced to death were left to hang until their bones turned white. By the 1840s the colony, fearing invasion, had converted the island into a fort and by 1857 the fort was manned and there were two 10-inch guns and twelve 32-pounders. The guns are now only fired during ceremonies and on special occasions. The island offers an interesting insight into Sydney's past and an excellent and unusual vantage point to view the city and the harbour foreshores. There are guided tours at 10:15, 12:15 and 14:00, and these can be booked by contacting the Maritime Services Board on tel: (02) 9240-2036.

Harbour Cruises ✱✱✱

There are over 30 cruises on Sydney Harbour. Not only does this offer extraordinary variety but, in a highly competitive market, shows that just about every visitor must be taking at least one cruise around the harbour.

The cruises depart from Circular Quay and Darling Harbour starting from 09:30 and continuing throughout the day until the night-time cruises which leave from 17:00 and the last return is around 22:30. They range from no frills, no need to book, tours around the harbour foreshores in well-equipped purpose-built cruise vessels, to catamarans, paddle-steamers, hydrofoils, a 1902 topsail schooner called *Solway Lass* and a re-creation of the sailing ship *Bounty* which was used in the Mel Gibson film of *Mutiny on the Bounty*.

Equally they range from simple tours around the harbour to tours including lunch, an evening meal, a Dixieland jazz band, a showboat with cabaret, a dinner and dance, and cuisine which ranges from carvery to Devonshire teas and Japanese and Asian dishes. There is every kind of cruise for every kind of budget and taste.

The sensible way to book is to contact the **Quayside Booking Centre**, either at No.2 wharf at Circular Quay (07:30–19:00) or Shop 208 on Manly Wharf (10:00–18:00). They are booking agents for all the major cruise operators and do not charge a booking fee. Both locations are open seven days a week and can be contacted on tel: (02) 9247-5151.

Cruises up the Parramatta River ***

Most of the ferries operating on Sydney Harbour move from one deepwater wharf across the harbour to another deepwater wharf. For a true change of pace, and something very different, take the **RiverCat** from Circular Quay to Parramatta. This is a journey which was commonplace for the early explorers and settlers who, without good roads, preferred to sail west up the harbour and enter the Parramatta River. The journey has become so popular on weekends that, if possible, it is better to make the trip during the week. Apart from the RiverCat, **Matilda Cruises** provide a leisurely journey up the river which includes both morning coffee and lunch. More details are available from tel: (02) 9264-7377.

For timetables and the best times to travel on the RiverCat, contact either the Parramatta Visitors Centre (tel: (02) 9630-3703) or the State Transit Infoline (tel: 13 1500). It is possible to buy a Sydney Pass for three, five or seven days on Sydney public transport which includes journeys on the RiverCat.

> **UNUSUAL CRUISES ON SYDNEY HARBOUR**
>
> There are a number of unusual ways to experience the beauty of Sydney Harbour beyond the usual round of cruise ships. If you're looking for something different, try:
> • **Sail Sydney:** a 90-minute or three-hour sailing adventure in Sydney Harbour with Australian Yachting Federation instructors. Tours leave from the Australian National Maritime Museum, Darling Harbour. For bookings, tel: (02) 9907-0004.
> • **Sydney Showboat:** a 90-minute cruise during the day and a 2½ hour cruise at night on an old paddle-steamer. The luncheon cruise features a Dixieland jazz band and the evening cruise is a cabaret/dinner outing. Tours leave from Campbell's Cove, The Rocks. For bookings, tel: (02) 9552-2722.
> • **Sea Dragon:** 9.6m sailboat which is an experience limited to only 20 people which will stop at harbour beaches for a barbeque. Tours leave from Campbell's Cove, The Rocks. For bookings, tel: 015 234 659.

Left: *There are literally dozens of cruises available on Sydney Harbour, including specialist trips around the foreshores and night cruises that feature cabaret acts and jazz bands.*

4
The Suburbs

Sydney is a vast collection of suburbs. Although the city has only a little over 3.7 million residents, in area it is nearly as large as Greater London. This is because Sydneysiders have always believed it is their birthright to own their own home. In recent times this has meant building a single-storey bungalow-style house on a 'quarter acre' block of land. They have accomplished this by moving further and further from the centre of the city; an 'urban sprawl'.

A careful observer can detect different types of housing as the city has expanded. Up until the 1880s the city was contained to what is now known as the 'inner city area', an area characterized by terrace houses (one- and two-storey) in the working class areas and rather grand houses either on hills or in positions which enjoy views across the harbour.

Between 1890 and 1910 a major period of suburban building saw the development of suburbs characterized by full-brick, federation-style houses. This style of housing continued until World War II when cheap housing sprang up within the city's western and southern suburbs the construction of vast numbers of fibro and weatherboard dwellings.

By the 1950s the dominant domestic house was the famous 'triple-fronted brick veneer'. By the late 1960s this was replaced by 'the project home', a style of house which was designed to be modified into a three-, four- or five-bedroom model. This style still dominates in the city's outer suburbs.

Don't Miss

*** Pittwater and Palm Beach: an hour's drive from the city, but a wonderful day's excursion.
** Hunters Hill: a truly beautiful harbour suburb with many fine old sandstone houses.
** Balmoral Beach: a delightful beach designed for promenading and enjoying the view out to the Heads.
** Watsons Bay: a range of interesting views of the city, the harbour and the Pacific all in close proximity.

Opposite: *Sydney's internationally famous Bondi Beach.*

Below: *One of Sydney's
most chic suburban shopping
centres, Double Bay in the
city's suburbs is a mixture
of European-style coffee
houses, exclusive boutiques
and antiquarian booksellers.*

Visitors interested in exploring and experiencing
Sydney's suburbia should simply get in a car and drive
in any direction. A few hours of turning off the main
arteries (most of Sydney is laid out in a grid pattern and
it is therefore quite difficult to get lost) and driving
down suburban streets will quickly give the curious visitor a feel for Sydney's distinctive domestic architecture
and the pre-eminence of the city's suburban lifestyle.

DOUBLE BAY *

No visit to Sydney would be complete without a trip to
Double Bay, one of Sydney's eastern suburbs which is
noted for its self-conscious sophistication and overtly
European ambience. The suburb's style is largely a result
of large numbers of Eastern Europeans moving into the
area from the 1950s onwards. Double Bay, Bellevue Hill,
Vaucluse and Point Piper has always been an area where
members of the city's elite lived, but the arrival of
wealthy Eastern Europeans saw the development of a
distinctive café society with many hotels and restaurants
offering outdoor, on-street tables.

Double Bay is a shopping centre noted for its designer clothes shops, bookshops, antique dealers and interi-
or decorators, and its excellent local cinema which commonly shows popular art movies. In recent times it has
tried, successfully, to maintain a 'village' atmosphere.

Although harbour swim-
ming has declined in the past
20 years (largely due to a fear
of pollution), there are two
excellent harbour swimming
areas near Double Bay –
Seven Shillings Beach and
Redleaf Pool. Double Bay is
reached by taking a train to
Edgecliff and walking down
the hill, by taxi – it is only 4km
(2 miles) east of the city – or
by a number of buses, including the Bondi & Bay Explorer.

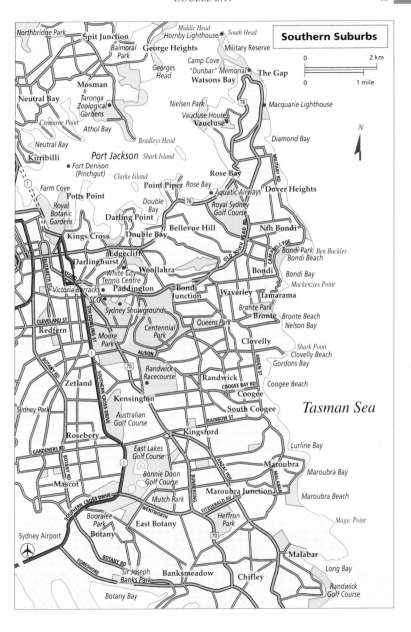

Southern Suburbs

Northbridge Park
Spit Junction
Middle Head
Hornby Lighthouse
South Head
Balmoral Park
George Heights
Military Reserve
Georges Head
Camp Cove
"Dunbar" Memorial
The Gap
Watsons Bay
Mosman
Taronga Zoological Gardens
Neutral Bay
Nielsen Park
Macquarie Lighthouse
Cremorne Point
Athol Bay
Vaucluse House
Vaucluse
Neutral Bay
Bradleys Head
Diamond Bay
Kirribilli
Port Jackson
Shark Island
Fort Denison (Pinchgut)
Clarke Island
Rose Bay
Farm Cove
Point Piper
Rose Bay
Dover Heights
Potts Point
Royal Botanic Gardens
Double Bay
Aquatic Airways
Darling Point
Royal Sydney Golf Course
Kings Cross
Double Bay
Bellevue Hill
Nth Bondi
Edgecliff
Campbell Pde
Bondi Park
Ben Buckler
Bondi Beach
Darlinghurst
Woollahra
White City Tennis Centre
Bondi
Bondi Bay
Victoria Barracks
Paddington
Bondi Junction
Mackenzies Point
SCG
Waverley
Tamarama
Sydney Showgrounds
Bronte Park
Moore Park
Queens Park
Bronte
Bronte Beach
Nelson Bay
Centennial Park
Redfern
Clovelly
Shark Point
Clovelly Beach
Gordons Bay
Zetland
Randwick Racecourse
Randwick
Coogee Bay Rd
Coogee Beach
Kensington
Coogee
Tasman Sea
Sydney Park
Australian Golf Course
South Coogee
Rainbow St
Rosebery
Kingsford
Lurline Bay
East Lakes Golf Course
Maroubra
Maroubra Bay
Bonnie Doon Golf Course
Mascot
Maroubra Junction
Maroubra Beach
Mutch Park
Booralee Park
Heffron Park
Magic Point
East Botany
Botany
Malabar
Sydney Airport
Sir Joseph Banks Park
Banksmeadow
Chifley
Long Bay
Botany Bay
Randwick Golf Course

0   2 km
0   1 mile

N

VAUCLUSE
Vaucluse House **

Easily accessible both by regular Sydney tours and the Bondi & Bay Explorer (it is stop 8 on the circular route), **Vaucluse House** is about 10km (6 miles) from the city centre. Set in gracious grounds, the original house was built in the early years of the 19th century by Sir Thomas Henry Brown Hayes. Sir Thomas was a larger-than-life character who had been transported as a convict because he had kidnapped the woman he loved, the daughter of a wealthy Irish banker.

The house was taken over by Captain John Piper (after whom Point Piper was named) in 1822, and in 1827 it was purchased by the famous explorer **William Charles Wentworth** (one of the trio who first crossed the Blue Mountains) who carried out extensive renovations and modifications and lived in the house until 1853. It is likely that the first cabinet meeting of the newly enfranchised government of New South Wales was held at Vaucluse House in 1856.

The house is much more than a reminder of the early history of Sydney. It is a beautifully preserved Sydney colonial residence, and the rooms are furnished with superb pieces from the period. Visitors can experience the luxury of the house and its gardens and walk through the gardens to the edge of the harbour. The **Vaucluse House Tea Rooms** offer fine food and are often used for weddings which are held in the gardens.

The grounds are open 08:00–17:00 daily and the house is open 10:00–16:45. This is a rare opportunity to experience what life in Sydney's eastern suburbs was like for the colony's elite in the middle of the 19th century. For more information, tel: (02) 9337-1957.

LIGHTHOUSES AT SOUTH HEAD

When the sailing ship *Dunbar* mistook The Gap for Sydney Heads and was wrecked with the loss of 120 lives, it was decided to build Hornby Light on the tip of South Head. This was not the first lighthouse to be built on the headland. As early as 1790 a signal station was established to indicate the location of the new settlement to ships which did not realize that the colony had moved from Botany Bay to Sydney Harbour. In 1818 the convict architect Francis Greenway completed the Macquarie Light which remained until the present light, which stands at the top of the hill above The Gap, was completed in 1883.

WATSONS BAY

Stop 9 on the Bondi & Bay Explorer, Watsons Bay is the furthest you can drive towards South Head, and is one of the most interesting areas in the Eastern Suburbs.

Watson's Bay Park ★★

The centrepoint is **Watsons Bay Park**, which is where the buses from the city centre terminate. This delightful park runs down to the water's edge. There are a couple of restaurants, a hotel and a takeaway all within close proximity. The most famous of the restaurants is **Doyles**, internationally renowned as one of Sydney's finest seafood eateries. There can be few more pleasant experiences than to sit at Doyles and gaze across the harbour at sunset while eating fresh lobster. If you want a cheaper option, with food which is nearly as good as the restaurant, the takeaway at the wharf offers a range of fresh seafood ideal for a picnic on the beach or in the park.

The Gap ★

If you are interested in sightseeing, walk up the hill to **The Gap** (the distance between the harbour and the Pacific is only a short walk). For years The Gap had a macabre reputation as a place to commit suicide. More recently it has attracted walkers. Nearby is the anchor from the *Dunbar* which, on 20 August 1857, mistook The Gap for the entrance to Sydney Harbour and was wrecked on the rocks with only one survivor.

Opposite: *Located in the exclusive suburb of Vaucluse, Vaucluse House is a beautiful 19th-century residence set in gardens which run down to the Sydney Harbour foreshore. It is now open to the public and, in recent times, the gardens have become a popular venue for weddings.*
Left: *Watsons Bay is known to Sydneysiders because of Doyles, the city's most famous fish restaurant, its excellent harbour beach and park, and the lighthouse which stands on the cliffs warning shipping of the dangers of 'The Gap'.*

BONDI BEACH

Bondi Beach probably gets its name from the Aboriginal word *boondi* which means 'the sound of waves breaking on a beach'. One of the suburb's early 'characters' was a man known as Nosey Bob who, in the 1880s, was the official hangman in New South Wales. He was known as Nosey Bob because a horse had kicked his nose in. He was such a strange character that the local publican used to break every glass Nosey Bob drank out of, claiming that no one else would drink from the glasses.

BONDI
Bondi Beach **

Sydney's most famous beach, **Bondi Beach** has come to symbolize the Australian way of life. The reality is that Bondi, which lies 7km (4 miles) east of the city, was the city's most popular beach from the 1890s until the 1950s because it was well serviced by trams and, for people living in the inner city areas, it was readily accessible.

Early images of Bondi are decidedly European in flavour. In the 1890s the beach had a huge aquarium. In the 1930s there were deckchairs spread from one end of the beach to the other and, on weekends, the beach was packed with holidaymakers and sunlovers.

By the 1960s Bondi was in decline. The old seafront buildings were fading, and access to the less crowded beaches north of Manly was such that they offered a better 'day out' option.

In recent times the beachfront has gone through a metamorphosis. Bondi is once again a fashionable address. The apartments and home units which characterize much of the suburb have been occupied by young people who enjoy the 'inner city' feel of the suburb. The promenade area along **Campbell Parade** has changed from a place which once offered only milk shakes, ice creams, hot dogs and pies, to a sophisticated café atmosphere where fast food outlets mix with good quality restaurants.

Below: *Bondi is the city's most popular summer destination. On a summer's day thousands of people rush to the beach seeking relief from the city's heat and humidity.*

A strange relic of past times occurs each Christmas Day when young English tourists, unaware that most Sydneysiders never spend Christmas Day on Bondi Beach, gather to celebrate a hot, sunny Christmas on the beach. Meanwhile most Sydneysiders are inside having a traditional English meal of turkey and Christmas pudding.

RANDWICK
Randwick Racecourse *

For people eager to 'have a flutter' on the horses, a visit to **Randwick Racecourse** can be a pleasant way to spend a day, particularly during the spring and autumn racing seasons. Sydneysiders have always had a passion for both horse racing and gambling. The colony's first racecourse was built on the present site of Hyde Park and the first race meeting was held in 1810. The **Australian Jockey Club** was formed in 1842, and by 1860 regular race meetings were being held at Randwick. There is still a sense of a family day out about the races. They are an integral part of the city's social calendar. The course is only 5km (3 miles) from the city centre and can be reached by a number of buses. Taxis are relatively inexpensive. For information about racing programs, both the Sydney daily papers – the *Sydney Morning Herald* and the *Daily Telegraph* – provide detailed form guides and race starting times.

EASTERN SUBURBS BEACHES

Although Bondi is Sydney's most famous beach, and North Shore partisans will argue that the city's northern beaches are superior, the beaches of the city's eastern and southern suburbs each have their own appeal.

Above: The beautifully laid out track and fields of the Randwick Racecourse.

> **ST MARKS, DARLING POINT**
>
> St Marks Church of England at Darling Point is known as Sydney's 'society' church. It was designed by Edmund Blacket, who designed the central buildings of Sydney University. Building started in 1848 and wasn't completed until 1870, when the spire was finally added. It is still the site of many of Sydney's most prestigious weddings and, famously, was the setting for Elton John's wedding.

A car journey from Bondi to Botany Bay is an adventure. There is no clearly defined coastal road, and the suburban development is such that driving around the beaches is a complex obstacle course.

Unlike the northern beaches, which can often be very long, the southern beaches are tiny and often nestled between narrow headlands. The exceptions are **Bondi**, **Coogee** and **Maroubra**. It is worth exploring the area and discovering the charms of such tiny beaches as **Tamarama**, **Bronte**, **Clovelly** and **Gordon's Bay**. This lack of large beaches is often compensated by rock pools and baths which are located at the water's edge, such as at the southern end of Bondi and Bronte and the northern end of Coogee. Of particular interest at Coogee are **Wylie's Baths**, which lie below the headland and beyond the southern end of the beach.

Opposite: *The northern shore of Sydney Harbour is a combination of a series of headlands interspersed with small inlets and bays. These are the suburbs of Mosman, Cremorne, Neutral Bay, Kirribilli and Milsons Point.*
Below: *Tamarama beach, south of Bondi, nestles between headlands.*

THE NORTH SHORE

The North Shore comprises suburbs west to Gladesville Bridge, north to Hornsby, and east to the Pacific Ocean. Sydney's lower North Shore is a mixture of tourist entertainment, historic buildings, distinctive suburbs, and excellent walking tracks around the harbour foreshores.

Many of the city's lower North Shore suburbs are of considerable historical interest. **Mosman** and **Clifton Gardens**, for example, have some of the finest Queen Anne Mansions in Sydney, and **Balmoral Beach** is an urban harbourside beach with a long, peaceful promenade edged by Moreton bay fig trees. At weekends, Balmoral is alive with inner city dwellers, many of whom come to the beach and organize huge, extended-family picnics on the lawns beside the promenade.

North Sydney to Mosman

A sensible short journey of exploration on the lower North Shore starts at North Sydney. Over the past 20 years Sydney's central business district has spread across the harbour so that high-rise office blocks, chic wine bars and fashionable eateries extend from Milsons Point up the ridge to North Sydney, which has become the city's centre for the computer technology and advertising industry.

It is an attractive centre which, under a benign local council, has managed to establish a distinctive identity which is characterized by its charming bush shelters and a strong sense of open space.

Beyond the office blocks, further up Miller Street, is **North Sydney Oval** which has been revitalized in such a way as to evoke a kind of 1930s charm. Turn into Military Road, which passes through the suburbs of **Neutral Bay** and **Cremorne** before reaching **Mosman** and the slopes of **Balmoral**. Two of tourist attractions in these suburbs are Nutcote and Taronga Park Zoo.

Nutcote *

A curious by-way of Australian literature, **Nutcote** is the home of the Australian children's author and illustrator May Gibbs. Located at 5 Wallaringa Avenue, Neutral Bay,

---

EATING ON MILITARY ROAD

From Neutral Bay, through Cremorne to Mosman, Military Road offers some of the best food on the lower North Shore.

• **Boronia House**, 624 Military Rd, Mosman, tel: (02) 9969-2099. Interesting mix of cultures and tastes.

• **The Pig & The Olive**, 318a Military Rd, Cremorne, tel: (02) 9953-7512, The ultimate pizza parlour.

• **Sala Thai**, 778 Military Rd, Mosman, tel: (02) 9969-9379. One of the oldest and best Thai restaurants in Sydney.

• **Rattlesnake Grill**, 130 Military Rd, Neutral Bay, tel: (02) 9953-4789. Specializing in North American cuisine from Cajun to chillies.

• **Viet Nouveau**, 731 Military Rd, Mosman, tel: (02) 9968-3548. Classic Vietnamese food with a strong French influence.

the gardens were the inspiration for her delightful and truly Australian collection of characters which include the Gumnut Babies and the Banksia Men. The house is a pleasant 15-minute ferry ride from Circular Quay to Hayes Street Wharf, and from there a five-minute walk up the hill. The house is now a gallery of Gibbs' original drawings and the view across the harbour from here is superb. For more information, tel: (02) 9953-4453. Open 11:00–15:00 Wednesday–Sunday.

Taronga Park Zoo ★★★

The zoo is located on the foreshore at the end of Bradleys Head Road in Mosman. It was opened in 1916 and on 24 September of that year the first ferry from Circular Quay to the zoo carried an elephant named Jessie. Soon after a regular passenger ferry service was established.

Voted the best international zoo in 1992, Taronga Park Zoo has superb views over Sydney Harbour and a substantial collection of Australian native fauna. The zoo can be reached by ferry from Wharf No.2, Circular Quay (the journey takes 12 minutes) or by bus from the bus terminals at Wynyard or St Leonards railway stations. There are two government transport travel passes available – the **Zoopass**, which combines ferry, bus and zoo admission and is available at Circular Quay, and **Zoolink**, which includes rail, ferry, bus and zoo admission and is available from suburban railway stations.

Below: *Taronga Zoo is one of the world's most beautifully located zoological parks. Visitors can inspect a wide range of Australian fauna, including the rarely seen platypus and koala as well as species from all the continents of the world.*

Displays include animals from all over the world, as well as echidnas, dingoes, wombats, kangaroos, wallabies, snakes and spiders. The koala walkabout and platypus exhibit offer opportunities to study creatures which few Australians have seen in the wild. For more information, tel: (02) 9969-2777. Open 9:00–17:00 daily.

North Sydney to Gladesville

Heading west from North Sydney are the harbourside suburbs of Waverton, Greenwich, Northwood, Longueville, Riverview, Hunters Hill and Gladesville. There are many beautiful parks along the foreshores of these suburbs, easily accessible by ferry, but the real attraction is the houses, some quaint, some old and grand, some large and modern, all interesting.

Hunter's Hill **

The land on this peninsula was sold between 1835 and 1843 and consequently this isolated suburb offers some of the finest 19th-century stone cottages and mansions in the Sydney suburban area. Many of the houses were built by brothers Jules and Didier Jourbert who bought 80ha (200 acres) and employed 70 Italian stonemasons to build a number of elegant residences. Hunter's Hill is also the main starting off point for the National Parks and Wildlife mammoth 250km (160 miles) 14-day trek – The Great North Walk – which runs through all the national parks from Sydney to Newcastle.

North Sydney to Hornsby

The Pacific Highway, which winds north from North Sydney, passes through a number of major shopping centres (notably the shopping centres of Chatswood and Gordon) before reaching the upper North Shore.

Castlecrag **

A little east of the highway is one of the few planned suburbs in Sydney. In the 1920s the American architect **Walter Burley Griffin** (the man who designed Canberra) subdivided the **Castlecrag** area and tried to develop an entire suburb which would look like a medieval castle. He planned to build modern sandstone houses on streets which stretched around the suburb like paths around the edges of a castle. A few of Burley Griffin's original houses remain. The one feature which persists is the suburb's street names – The Bulwark, Redoubt, Bastion, The Scarp, The Barricade, Citadel,

---

HOMES IN HUNTERS HILL

Of particular interest in Hunters Hill are:
• **Fig Tree House**, 1 Reiby Rd. It incorporates part of the house the convict businesswoman Mary Reibey built in 1836.
• **St Claire**, 2 Wybalena Rd. Considered one of the finest stone houses in the suburb.
• **Clifton**, 7 Woolwich Rd. A two-storey mansion built in 1891. The sandstone was quarried on the site.
• **Town Hall**, Alexandra St. Built in 1856 and one of the suburb's most prominent landmarks.

SYDNEY HARBOUR

Sydney Harbour is regarded as one of the safest harbours in the world. It covers an area of 5,504ha (13,600 acres) and more than half of the harbour is deeper than 9m (30ft). At its deepest point, just west of the Sydney Harbour Bridge, it is 47.2m (155ft) deep. This safety for ships does not extend to humans. The harbour is a breeding ground for sharks and it is foolish to swim in unprotected waters.

Above: *Sydney Harbour meets small freshwater rivers at a number of points. At Lane Cove National Park, a narrow weir divides the harbour from the Lane Cove River. People come here for picnics and relax beside the fresh water as swans glide by.*

Parapet and Rampart – reminiscent of an ancient castle. The plan was not successful. Today the suburb is noted for its exclusive housing and excellent views across Middle Harbour.

Lane Cove ★★★

A pleasant escape from the city can be enjoyed by travelling to the **Lane Cove National Park** (just west of Chatswood) which offers numerous bushwalks and pleasant picnic spots beside the Lane Cove River. A riverboat runs along the river taking in the surrounding bushland sights, and row boats can be hired as a delightful, self-powered alternative.

Upper North Shore ★★

This is an area of considerable old-wealth and charm. it is about as close as Sydney gets to the Hollywood hills with suburbs like **Killara**, **Pymble**, **St Ives**, **Wahroonga** and **Gordon**. Here large houses have been built on huge blocks of land.

The upper North Shore was first settled along the ridge, which also happens to be the route of the railway line. By the 1960s, houses were being built in the gullies on either side of the ridge. Thus the places close to the railway line tend to be older. The main characteristic of these suburbs is the way they have managed to mix the Australian bush (there are gum trees everywhere) with a distinctively English ambience created by deciduous trees which turn the area into a wonderland of colour in the autumn.

Like so much of suburban Sydney, the best way to discover the elegance and wealth of the upper North Shore is to simply head off to the east of the railway line (there is a clear demarcation here – east of the railway line is more chic than west) at a suburb like Pymble or Wahroonga and explore the back streets. This is an area where many of the city's successful professionals and executives live.

THE NORTHERN BEACHES

Sydneysiders will argue about their beaches forever. The truth is that the city is blessed with an excess of great beaches and that favourites are usually determined by childhood memories rather than any objective criteria. The northern beaches from Manly to Palm Beach each have their own particular appeal.

Manly **

After Bondi, Manly is Sydney's most famous beach. Located on an isthmus just north of North Head, the suburb's appeal is based partly on the way that most people arrive and partly on the fact that there are only a few hundred metres between the harbour and the ocean.

There can be few more pleasant journeys on public transport than the ferry trip from Circular Quay to Manly Wharf. The journey down Sydney Harbour and across the heads is breathtaking and, on a stormy day, the waves coming through the Head can add a sense of drama and excitement as the vessel pitches in the swell.

Manly is geared for visitors. The centrepiece is a short walk along **The Corso**, the main street, to the beach. The street is a mixture of gift shops, fast food eateries and typical beach activities. The mall area is alive with buskers and there is plenty of free entertainment for children.

> **HISTORIC HOMES**
>
> Visitors wanting to explore Sydney's most interesting historic homes can purchase a 'Ticket Through Time' which is valid for three months and provides entry to seven of Sydney's most interesting historic homes, including the Rose Seidler House at 71 Clissold Rd, Wahroonga. The Rose Seidler House, which was built in 1948-50, was the first uncompromisingly modern house in Sydney. It is open for inspection on Sundays between 10.30–16.00. The 'Ticket Through Time' can be purchased by contacting tel: (02) 9692-8366.

Left: *The walk from Manly Wharf, which is on the harbour side, to Manly Beach is a popular promenade for visitors to this suburb.*

SEEING MANLY

There are a number of tours available around Manly. If you prefer to be shown the sights rather than wandering around the streets and beaches, the following businesses provide good services:
• **Manly Sightseeing/ North Head Shuttle Bus**, tel: (02) 9938-4677.
• **Manly In-Sight Tours**, tel: (02) 9905-1350.
• **Manly Daily Trackless Train**, tel: 018 046 910.
• **Boomerang Bus Tours**, tel: (02) 9913-8402.
For general bookings in the area try the **Quayside Booking Service**, located at Manly Wharf, tel: (02) 9977-5296.

Northern Suburbs

Mooney Mooney · Spectacle Is. · Brisbane Water National Park · Umina · Wagstaffe · Bouddi N.P.
Marramarra National Park · Dangar Is. · Long Is. · Hawkesbury · River Cruises · Pearl Beach
Muogamarra Nature Reserve · Brooklyn · Patonga · Lion Island
0 3 km
0 1 mile
Cowan · Cowan Creek · Lookout · Broken Bay · Aboriginal Engravings · Barrenjoey Lighthouse · Commodore Heights · Nth Palm Beach
Berowra Waters · Ku-ring-gai Chase National Park · WEST HEAD RD · Palm Beach · Little Head · Whale Beach
Berowra Heights · Berowra · Lovett Bay · Lookout · Clareville · Avalon
Berowra Valley Bushland · Ku-ring-gai Chase National Park · Aboriginal Engravings · Scotland Is. · Church Point · Avalon Beach · Bilgola · Newport · Newport Beach
Bobbin Head · Bayview · Bungan Beach
Visitors Centre · Duffys Forest · Ingleside · Mona Vale · Mona Vale Beach · Warriewood Beach
Asquith · Waratah Park · Terrey Hills · Warriewood · Turimetta Beach
Hornsby · Wildflower Garden · Elanora Heights · Garigal National Park · North Narrabeen Beach
Nth St.Ives · Narrabeen · Narrabeen Beach
Wahroonga · St.Ives · Garigal National Park · Cromer · Collaroy Beach
Turramurra · Belrose · Long Reef Point · Long Reef Beach
Pymble · Dee Why · Dee Why Beach · Wingala
Gordon · Brookvale · Curl Curl Beach
Kilara · Killarney Heights · Harbord Beach · Queenscliff Beach
Chatswood · Castlecove · Manly · Manly Beach
North Ryde · Northbridge · The Spit · North Head
Lane Cove

N

Below: *Oceanworld offers a fascinating insight into an underwater world, and is one of Manly's most popular attractions.*

On the beachfront between the Corso and the surf is the **Manly Vsitors Information Centre** (Tel: (02) 9977-1088), with information on tours, festivals, restaurants and accommodation as well as the area's major attractions – the **Waterworks** (take your swimming costume) and **Oceanworld** (an aquarium specializing in sharks and stingrays an opportunity to dive in among them). The best visit to Manly will always be the one focusing on sightseeing, swimming and walking along the beach.

Quarantine Station *

A highlight of Manly must be a trip to the Quarantine Station and a walk around North Head which, arguably, offers the best views of Sydney Harbour. It is a half-hour walk from Manly Wharf. The best way of travelling to the area is by the **North Head Shuttle Bus** which leaves from the wharf. The Quarantine Station was used for over a century to house migrants who arrived in Australia carrying, or suspected of carrying, dangerous diseases. It is an interesting collection of old wooden buildings.

Nearby is the **North Fort Artillery Museum** (tel: (02) 9976-1138). The museum is located in this scenic park because of the interesting 19th-century gun emplacements and the long association North Head has with the protection of the city.

Sydney Harbour National Park ***

A series of paths and vantage points offer superb views up the harbour towards the city, south to South Head and the city's Eastern Suburbs and, far below, to the Pacific Ocean which beats relentlessly on the cliffs of North Head. This area is now part of Sydney Harbour National Park, and visitors curious about the flora which existed around Sydney Harbour before European settlement will find an array of hardy and colourful coastal plants.

Above: *Manly combines both a harbour beach and an ocean beach separated by an isthmus.*

FERRIES AND JETCATS

There is no need to book on either the Manly Ferry or the Manly JetCat. They both cross the harbour regularly. The following is a summary of the timetables:
• **Manly Ferry:** 06:00 to 9:00 – every 15 minutes, 09:00 to 17:00 – every 30 minutes. Last journey 19:00 from Circular Quay and 19:40 from Manly.
• **JetCat:** 06:00 to 10:25 – every 20-25 minutes, 10:50 to 16:20 – every 30 minutes. Last journey 23:50 from Circular Quay and 00:10 from Manly.

Above: *Some of Sydney's most popular beaches include Manly (pictured here), Dee Why, Narrabeen, Curl Curl, Avalon, Newport and Palm Beach.*

Manly to Newport ✭✭✭

Every Sydneysider has a favourite beach and with such a vast range of beautiful beaches to choose from, invariably opinion is based on childhood memories rather than objective criteria. Stretching north from Manly to Palm Beach each area has its own particular charm. From Manly the beaches, as they run north, include **North Steyne** and **Queenscliff** (which are both part of the extended Manly Beach which is uninterrupted from Fairy Bower to the headland at Queenscliff). Then come **Freshwater**, North and South **Curl Curl**, **Dee Why** (a beach which is separated narrowly from the Dee Why Lagoon which lies behind it) and **Long Reef Beach** which edges the southern boundary of the picturesque Long Reef Golf Course. To the north of the Long Reef headland lies Collaroy Basin (sometimes known as Fishermans Beach) and the long, straight stretch of beach which has been broken up into **Collaroy** and **Narrabeen**. (Narrabeen is separated from Narrabeen Lake – the mouth of the lake lies to the north of the beach.)

North of Narrabeen lies the small and inaccessible **Turimetta Beach** (Little Narrabeen) which does not have a life-saving club, and the beautiful **Warriewood** Beach. Beyond is the long **Mona Vale** Beach which is also backed by a golf course and has an attractive rock pool.

Beyond Mona Vale are the peninsula beaches, some of which are inaccessible and so highly prized by people seeking privacy from the masses who drive to the beaches in summer. **Bungan Beach** can only be reached by walkways, **Bilgola** is nestled below Barrenjoey Road, and you almost need a street directory to find **Whale Beach**.

The more accessible beaches are **Newport**, a popular and fashionable beach for the North Shore's wealthy residents, **Avalon** and magnificent **Palm Beach** – part of one of the city's most exclusive belts and holiday retreat (and, in some cases, permanent home) of the city's elite.

THE NEWPORT ARMS

One of Sydney's most famous pubs is the Newport Arms, a charming watering hole on the Pittwater side of Newport where, traditionally, yachting enthusiasts and people who have driven to the beach from the North Shore gather for Sunday lunch. The pub was made famous in the 1960s when an early edition of *Oz* magazine featured a cartoon by Martin Sharp titled 'The Word Flashed Around the Arms' – a satiric view of the social mores of the hotel at the time. The amusing sketch led to one of Sydney's most famous obscenity trials.

The whole area is a delight. The best way to visit it is to hire a car and simply explore at your leisure, stopping to admire the view, swimming in the numerous rock pools which have been cut into the rocky outcrops at the end of the beaches, or enjoying the summertime ambience of the suburban shopping centres which seem designed to sell beachwear, fast food and suntan lotions more than the ordinary needs of everyday life.

Of particular interest are the views afforded from the ridge that runs up the coast. This ridge is particularly impressive along the peninsula where the wonders of modern architecture and engineering find houses perched, implausibly, on the edges of cliffs. One of the highlights is the round trip from just beyond Avalon, where the visitor can follow Barrenjoey Road to Palm Beach (with Pittwater on the left) and then take the winding Florida Road and Whale Beach Road back along the coast where every turn brings another spectacular view and another million dollar mansion into view.

This is an area where swimming, walking and exploring are high on the list of enjoyable pastimes.

Pittwater and Palm Beach ★★★

Pittwater is a glorious expanse of water which lies at the northern end of Sydney's northern beaches. It was discovered by Governor Phillip in 1788 who named it after William Pitt the Younger. He declared it 'the finest piece of water which I ever saw . . . it would contain the navy of Great Britain'. Phillip would be amazed that a place he imagined containing the navy of Great Britain now contains only small pleasure craft and windsurfers. It is one of Sydney's most attractive retreats.

In theory, although most of the locals would disagree, Palm Beach and Pittwater are part of Sydney. In reality, the people

Below: *One of Sydney's most exclusive beach suburbs is Palm Beach, the last northern beach before the Hawkesbury River.*

Below: *At the northern
end of Palm Beach is the
Barrenjoey Lighthouse
which stands on a rocky
outcrop overlooking
Pittwater and the
Hawkesbury River. There
is a pleasant walk to the
lighthouse. The lighthouse
has top exceptional views
of the whole area.*

who live on 'the Peninsula' (as they call the area) think of
themselves as being distanced from what goes on far to
the south. Certainly, a trip to Palm Beach is not like visiting a beach in the Sydney metropolitan area. The traveller
drives forever up the northern beaches on a road which
winds backwards and forwards, crossing from ocean
beaches to quiet Pittwater retreats. The bus service from
the city takes over two hours.

There are a variety of things which await the visitor at
Palm Beach. The ferry trip across to **The Basin** is well
worth taking. On the Palm Beach side of Pittwater at
Snapperman Beach, there are a number of good fish
restaurants and fish and chip shops. The walk along the
isthmus and up to the lighthouse is well worth the effort
(the views across to **Lion Island** are superb). For the highly
regarded Sydney writer, Ruth Park, the reason for visiting
Palm Beach was 'to join the bodies lying motionless on the
singularly golden sand, stupefied with sun, staring
through their eyelids at the sky'. Those observations were
written in 1973. These days the threat of skin cancer and
excessive levels of ultraviolet rays have people rushing for
the 15+ sun lotion and seeking shade after a few minutes.

Barrenjoey Lighthouse ★★★

The walk up to Barrenjoey Lighthouse is rewarding. The
lighthouse was designed by the same architect who
designed the Sydney General Post Office. It was built in
1881 and, for years, operated as
a beacon for the river traffic
which plied the Hawkesbury
River and Broken Bay.

Millionaires and film and pop
stars have settled on the
Peninsula, and the views from
the houses they have built on the
cliffs at Palm Beach and Whale
Beach are spectacular. It is easy
to imagine that the lifestyle that
goes on inside these opulent
homes matches the view.

BOTANY BAY *

In 1938 a *Jubilee History of the Municipality of Botany* proudly declared: 'No spot in Australia is so rich in historical memories and memorial – the Tablet on the cliff fixed in 1823; the sandstone pillar, erected by the Hon. Thomas Holt in 1870, to mark Cook's landing place and the centenary of his arrival; the granite shaft to commemorate Dr. Solander, the Swedish Botanist; the memorial to ill-fated Farby Sutherland, the first British citizen to leave his bones in Australian soil; the stately column raised by the most patriotic of people, the French, to hallow the last spot on these shores touched by La Perouse.'

Botany Bay is steeped in the history of Sydney and Australia. It is hard now to imagine what it must have been like when Captain Cook first sailed into the bay in 1770 or when Captain Arthur Phillip and the First Fleet arrived offshore in 1788. A central feature of the bay is **Sydney Kingsford Smith Airport** with its extended runway jutting artificially out into the bay. At other points around the bay there is an oil refinery, and one of Sydney's largest container terminals. A distinctive Novotel hotel stands behind the beach at Brighton-le-Sands.

Above: *Built in Fremantle, this is an exact replica of the* HM *Barque* Endeavour *which Captain Cook sailed to Australia in a voyage which led to European settlement of Australia.*
Below: *Kingsford Smith Airport lies south of Sydney.*

SCOTLAND ISLAND

One of Sydney's best kept secrets is Scotland Island in Pittwater. This tiny island is home to a small number of people whose only contact with the outside world is by either rowing or sailing across to Church Point. It was first settled by Andrew Thompson in 1810 and subdivided in 1911. The island has five wharves – Tennis Court Wharf, Eastern Wharf, Carol's Wharf, Bell Wharf and Cargo Wharf. A local ferry service runs from Church Point, but many of the residents prefer to make their own way across the narrow stretch of water which separates the island from the mainland.

Opposite: *Parramatta was the first settlement after Sydney Cove and it has significant historic buildings including the Old Government House.*

A SEASIDE RESORT

While the French explorer La Perouse is closely tied to the history of Botany Bay, it is wrong to think of the beachside suburb of Brighton-le-Sands as having any French associations. The suburb came into existence in the 1880s when an enterprising local landowner decided to develop the western shore of Botany Bay. He named the location after the famous English seaside resort, Brighton. To distinguish it from the English Brighton he added 'le Sands'.

WATKIN TENCH AT BOTANY BAY

When Captain Cook first saw Botany Bay he described it as having 'some of the finest meadows in the world'. Captain Watkin Tench, left to explore the shoreline while Captain Arthur Phillip rowed north and found Sydney Harbour, described the shores of Botany Bay more accurately as shallow, sandy soil and spongy bog where men 'plunged knee-deep at every step'. No one has ever been able to explain why Cook described this sandy land as the 'finest meadows'.

Visitors who may be interested in looking at the more unusual aspects of Sydney can usefully spend half a day exploring the foreshores of Botany Bay. At the northeastern tip of the bay (at the southern end of Anzac Parade) is **Long Bay Gaol**, Sydney's major gaol, and **Prince Henry Hospital**. Behind these two rather severe institutions there are some lovely walks along the coast. Of particular interest is **Little Bay**, a charming retreat which the artist Christo 'wrapped up' with huge white sheets in the 1970s. This beautiful little bay is located behind Prince Henry Hospital. Further around the coast is the urban Aboriginal community of **La Perouse**. Each year on 26 January the community remembers the invasion of Australia by holding its own Australia Day celebrations with a concert which lasts for the entire day.

The other places of interest around the bay include numerous picnic spots and the protected bathing areas at **Brighton-le-Sands**, **Ramsgate** and **Dolls Point** (take special note of the shark signs beside the beach – it is not safe to swim in the unprotected waters of the bay); the delightful nature reserve at **Towra Point**, one of the southern headlands, which is home to birds which migrate from as far away as Japan and Siberia; and the southern headland where Captain Cook, on 1 April 1770, stepped onto Australian soil for the first time. It is said that Cook rowed ashore with a small group and when they approached **Kurnell** he said 'Jump out, Isaac!' to his young nephew. The boy obeyed, thus making him the first known European to set foot on the coast of eastern Australia.

There is an obelisk commemorating the event, and nearby there is a stone with the inscription, 'Forby Sutherland. A seaman on the Endeavour under Captain Cook. The first British subject to die in Australia was buried here. 1st May (Log Date) 2nd May (Calendar Date) 1770.' Sutherland, who died of tuberculosis, gave his name to the shire which stretches south and includes the beachside suburb of **Cronulla** which lies to the south of Kurnell.

HISTORIC PARRAMATTA **

Parramatta is the geographical centre of Sydney. It is a thriving suburban centre, connected to Sydney's central business district by the RiverCat and train. It is the hub of a huge area of Sydney's western, southwestern and north-western suburbs and is serviced by a large number of private bus companies.

Within weeks of the arrival of the First Fleet in Sydney Cove, expeditions had reached the present site of Parramatta and it was agreed that the fertile soils of the area would be ideal for crops and vegetable gardens. By November 1788 **Rose Hill**, just east of the present site of Parramatta, was chosen as the second settlement site in the Sydney basin. Within a year, grain had been successfully grown and by 1791 the area had been renamed 'Parramatta', an Aboriginal word which may mean either 'the place where the eels lie down' or 'the head of the river'.

HISTORIC PARRAMATTA

There are over 40 sites of historic importance in the Parramatta area. These include Old Government House, Elizabeth Farm and Experiment Farm, as well as:
- **Hambledon Cottage**, 63 Hassell St, (open 11:00-16:00 Wednesday, Thursday, weekends) tel: (02) 9635-6924. Built in 1824 by John Macarthur.
- **Brislington**, Marsden St, (open 10:30-16:00 Sundays only) tel: (02) 9630-3703. Built in 1821.
- **Roseneath**, cnr Ross & O'Connell Sts. Built in 1837 for a widow who had arrived in the colony with nine children and 63 merino sheep.
For those tourists who are interested, Parramatta also has a number of historic cemeteries.

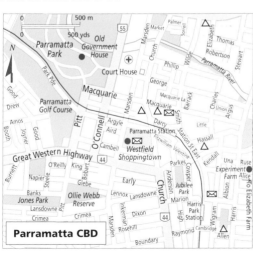

Parramatta CBD

The area is full of firsts. It was the site of the colony's first successful farm (at **Experimental Farm** an 1834 building on the original site can be inspected on Ruse Street – 10:00–16:00 Tue–Thur and 11:00–16:00 Sun, tel: (02) 9635-5655 for information), first vineyard, first legal brewery, orchard, tannery, gaol, ploughshed and race meeting.

Above: *Parramatta was the site of the city's first successful farm. In 1834 a building was constructed on the original site of Experimental Farm.*

HISTORY OF PENRITH

1789 Watkin Tench discovered the Nepean River and described it as 'nearly as broad as the Thames at Putney'.
1813 Blaxland, Wentworth and Lawson crossed the river at Emu Ford on their successful crossing of the Blue Mountains.
1815 The road through the Blue Mountains passed through the present site of Penrith.
1818 Governor Macquarie named the town after Penrith in England.
1851 The town grew as an important staging post to the goldfields.
Today Penrith is the western limit of Sydney's suburban sprawl.

Elizabeth Farm ★★

Elizabeth Farm (1793) at 70 Alice Street was built for John and Elizabeth Macarthur. John Macarthur founded Australia's hugely important merino sheep industry and was one of the country's most powerful early settlers. His heirs are about as close to an aristocracy as democratic Australia gets. The house still contains part of the oldest European building in the country. Its style – deep verandahs and an overhanging roof – was to become a standard for cool, rural residences for most of the 19th century (10:00–16:30 Tue–Sun). There is a tearoom which serves teas and lunch. For information, tel: (02) 9635-9488 .

Old Government House ★★

The residence of the colony's early governors, Old Government House is open between 10:00–16:00 on Tuesdays, Wednesdays and Thursdays and between 11:00–16:00 on Sundays. It is located in Parramatta Park. For more information: tel: (02) 9635-8149.

THE WESTERN SUBURBS

The Western Suburbs are the true Australian heartland. They stretch from Parramatta to the Blue Mountains, south to Campbelltown, and north to Richmond and Windsor. Although inner city dwellers tend to dismiss them as uninteresting suburbia, they are where most

Sydneysiders live. If you want to experience Sydney's suburbia, there are a number of attractions which are popular with the locals and are worth visiting.

Wonderland *

Australia's Wonderland is the country's largest theme park. It is of Disneyland scale with a Hanna Barbera Land, a Goldrush area which includes a huge wooden roller coaster and a 'Snowy River Rampage' whitewater adventure, Transylvania – with a Demon roller coaster which twists 360° – wildlife park, artificial beach, and an open-air theatre which offers a wide variety of entertainment. (Open weekends and during NSW school holidays 10:00–17:00 and later on Saturday nights in summer.) For more information, tel: (02) 9830-9100 or the 24-hour Info line tel: (02) 9832-1777.

Above: *Wonderland is a huge amusement park, with death-defying roller coaster rides and merry-go-rounds.*

Penrith *

Beyond Wonderland is Penrith, a thriving outer suburb which includes the huge **Panthers Resort**, Mulgoa Road, tel: (047) 21-7700. Built as part of the superstructure supporting the local football team, this resort is located on the Nepean River. Not only is it a hotel/motel, but it also offers a bewildering array of family entertainment from nightclubs to a water-ski park and numerous restaurants. Nearby is the **Museum of Fire** with its interesting displays of old fire engines, the **Joan Sutherland Performing Arts Centre** and the Nepean River which is the venue for the annual Head of the River rowing competition. Downriver from Penrith Panthers Resort is the **Nepean Belle Paddle Steamer** which provides cruises along the river and through the Nepean Gorge. For more information, tel: (047) 32-7671 for the local Tourist Information Centre or (047) 21-7700 for the Panthers World of Entertainment.

Beyond Penrith lie the Blue Mountains.

THE REGATTA

When Watkin Tench described the Nepean River at Penrith as 'nearly as broad as the Thames at Putney' he could not have imagined that, 200 years later, it would serve an equivalent function every year. Just as Oxford and Cambridge challenge each other to a rowing competition on the Thames near Putney so, each year, Sydney's GPS (Great Public Schools) challenge each other to the 'Head of the River'. The race is watched by thousands.

5
Trips around Sydney

Sydney is surrounded by interesting daytrips. It would be a rare visitor who did not travel either to the Blue Mountains, to the South Coast, to the National Parks which surround the city, or to the Central Coast. Each area has its own appeal. To the south of the city, the spectacular views available from the cliffs and the escarpment behind Greater Wollongong, are the best near Sydney. The **Blue Mountains**, with their deep box canyons, waterfalls and old-world charm, are dramatic and beautiful. The smudgy blue which rises from the gum trees is an aspect of the Australian 'bush' which every visitor to the country should experience. The national parks which edge **Broken Bay** and the **Hawkesbury River** offer many superb bushwalking trails and the tranquil waterways are ideal for boating and fishing. Further north, the beaches of the Central Coast are a reminder that commuting to Sydney can be a very tempting option.

Individual travellers will find the method of travelling they prefer. There are a wide range of organized daily trips offered by numerous tour operators. Public transport, particularly train travel, is fast and efficient. There are rail commuter services through the Blue Mountains, south to Wollongong and to the Central Coast. Hiring a car is a sensible option for visitors who want to explore on their own. In all cases a journey of around 100km (60 miles) – a total of 200–250km (120–150 miles) as a round trip – will get the visitor from the centre of the city to the major regions.

Opposite: *The majestic Blue Mountains lie to the west of Sydney.*

Opposite: *The Royal National Park lies south of Sydney. It is characterised by peaceful, isolated beaches and excellent bushwalks that allow visitors to experience the kind of flora, such as these Gymea lilies common in the Sydney basin before European settlement.*
Right: *Garie and Wattamolla Beaches lie within the boundaries of the Royal National Park. Both have excellent surfing and, in the case of Wattamolla, there is a delightful lagoon behind the beach which is ideal for children and family swimming.*

ROYAL NATIONAL PARK ★★★

The traveller leaving Sydney and heading south first comes to the Royal National Park which spreads from the beaches of Wattamolla and Garie through unspoilt coastal wilderness to the quiet waters of the Hacking River. Covering 14,969ha (37,000 acres) this glorious and diverse park lies less than 40km (25 miles) from the centre of Sydney. It was, in fact, Australia's first National Park and only the second in the world (Yellowstone in the USA was the first). It was dedicated by the government for rest and recreation, a purpose that has not changed for over 100 years.

The park was converted from a National Park to a 'Royal' National Park (a change which seemed very important at the time) after Queen Elizabeth II travelled through the park on her way to Wollongong in 1954.

While most visitors drive down the Princes Highway – the turn off to the park is 2.5km (1½ miles) south of Sutherland and 27km (17 miles) south from the city centre – it is possible to enter the park by ferry from **Cronulla**. The ferry from Cronulla to Bundeena operates between 05:00 and 19:00 daily and leaves every half-hour. Visitors travel across **Port Hacking** and arrive in the small township of Bundeena (it has a population of around 2500) which is located on the northern shoreline of the park.

Back to Nature

Most people who travel to the park have a specific leisure activity in mind. They may want to go surfing or lagoon swimming at **Wattamolla** or **Garie Beach**, or to do some quiet ocean fishing. They may simply want to have a picnic or spend a day rowing or paddling on the small lake above Audley Weir. Or, being keen bushwalkers, they may walk along some of the hundreds of bush trails which were developed in the park in the 1920s.

It does not matter what your favourite leisure activity is, the Royal National Park caters for just about every taste. The bushwalker can catch the **Bundeena** ferry and walk to **Jibbon Point** which is at the end of a 1km (0.5 miles) beach track from Bundeena. This walk passes some fascinating Aboriginal rock platform carvings of sea creatures. Given that most of the Aborigines had left the area nearly a century ago, and that just across the water the suburbs of modern Sydney can be seen, this is a reminder that long before Europeans arrived the Aborigines lived an idyllic life in this area.

Coast Track ***

For people who want to explore the coastline, there is the **Coast Track**, a marvellous 30km (19 miles) walk from Bundeena to Otford. The track runs the length of the park's sandstone cliff line, passing through Little Marley and Marley Beach, Wattamolla,

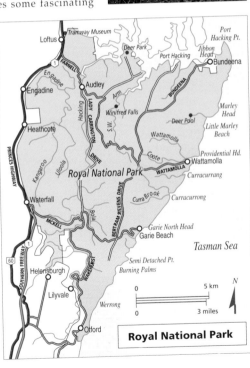

Burning Palms and Garie. It is too long to attempt in one day. Bushwalking enthusiasts tend to do the walk in two days, while daytrippers, happy to do the first section, walk for two hours, reach Little Marley and Marley Beach, and then return to Bundeena.

In winter and spring the low scrubland and heath is alive with magnificent wildflower displays. The smell of the flowers, the tang of the ocean winds, the sculptured sandstone of the headlands and caves, the sandy beaches, and the sounds of the birds, all make the Coast Walk unforgettable.

Above: *Surfers are always searching for the perfect wave. Many head towards the Royal National Park where the steep cliffs, lonely beaches and relentless Pacific Ocean combine to provide ideal surfing conditions.*

Marley Beach *

Day walkers should recognize that Marley Beach is dangerous for swimming (a characteristic of many of the beaches south of Sydney – be warned!) but **Little Marley Beach**, which is further south, is a popular swimming and fishing spot. Little Marley also offers a camping area and a freshwater stream. The walker can then take the track up onto the plateau and head back to Bundeena.

Flora and Fauna

Walkers who pass the freshwater swamps see Christmas Bells with their red and yellow flowers (they appear from December to February), Needlebush, Bottlebrush, Pink Swamp-heath, Coral Heath and paperbark shrub.

In the forests and woodlands the alert birdwatcher can see Wedge-tailed Eagles, Black-shouldered Kites, White-naped Honeyeaters, Crimson Rosellas, pee-wees, Red wattlebirds, Sulphur-crested Cockatoos and bronzewings. If you are very patient you might see satin bower-birds and lyrebirds in the rainforests. Around the swamps and lagoons the Azure Kingfisher, Welcome Swallow, New Holland Honeyeater and Pacific Black Duck can be seen.

SYDNEY'S PARKS AND GARDENS

The City of Sydney has 356ha (880 acres) of parks and gardens, and in the Sydney metropolitan area there are over 5700ha (14,000 acres) of parklands. To the south of the city the 14,969ha (37,000 acres) Royal National Park, which was created in 1879, was Australia's first 'National Park' and the second in the world after Yellowstone in the USA.

Native mammals include bush-rats, a range of gliders, bandicoots, Ringtail Possums, dunnarts, lizards and goannas. There are also snakes, and summer walkers should be careful, as many of them are poisonous. It is unlikely that day visitors will make contact with any of these animals.

Beaches

The beaches at **Garie**, **Burning Palms** and **Wattamolla** are exceptionally beautiful. Burning Palms, a hideout for fishermen since the turn of the century, has a number of cottages which have been tolerated by the park authorities. The entire 19km (12 miles) of coastline which forms the park's eastern boundary is noted for its excellent fishing.

Hacking River *

One of the park's most idyllic picnic spots is the grassy area south of the Audley Weir. Here, beside the dammed Hacking River, is a pleasant parkland where boats can be hired and picnics held under willow trees and beside the cool waters of the river. Such relaxation is far removed from the bustle of the city which lies to the north.

SOUTH TO WOLLONGONG
Stanwell Tops ***

The greatest reward of Sydney's south coast awaits those who travel right through the Royal National Park and, passing through **Otford**, arrive at **Stanwell Tops**. The view from Stanwell Tops is worth travelling all day for. On a clear day you can see down the coast to Wollongong. The jutting headlands of **Coalcliff**, **Scarborough** and **Clifton** make this ruggedly beautiful stretch of coastline one of the scenic jewels of the entire Australian east coast.

The **Coast Road** from Stanwell Tops to Wollongong is full of surprises. It starts with one of the most spectacular views on the entire east coast, moves through a series of old coal mining villages which cling to the edge of cliffs, reaches Thirroul where the English writer D.H. Lawrence spent over three months writing his famous novel *Kangaroo*, and then continues through Bulli before reaching the outer edges of New South Wales' third-largest city.

HISTORY OF THE ROYAL NATIONAL PARK

In 1879 Australia's first 'National Park' was established on a modest 7200ha (17,800 acres) south of Port Hacking. It was dedicated by the government as an area specifically for rest and recreation. The original idea was to create a large, open space for the future residents of Sydney. Certainly, when it was dedicated in 1879, someone observed that it should be 'a sanctuary for the pale-faced Sydneyites fleeing the pollution – physical, mental and social – of that closely-packed city'. In 1880 the area was doubled to 14,500ha (36,000 acres) and in 1934 the great NSW conservationist Myles Dunphy persuaded the government to add a further 520ha (1300 acres) of land around Garawarra. It became a 'Royal' National Park after Queen Elizabeth II travelled through it in 1954.

Above: *Spectacular views can be enjoyed from Bald Hill above Stanwell Park. Australian aviation inventor, Lawrence Hargrave, carried out his early experiments here in aerodynamics.*

Travelling from Sydney, Stanwell Tops can be reached by car. It is also possible to catch a train from Central Station, alight at **Stanwell Park** and walk up the road to **Bald Hill**.

Stanwell Park *

Stanwell Park is famous for its connections with the early history of aviation. The sleepy little beach resort below Bald Hill was once the home of **Lawrence Hargrave**, inventor of the box kite and one of the founding fathers of modern aviation. On top of Bald Hill there is a monument to Hargrave. Hang-glider enthusiasts use the hill as a launching point for their death-defying flights out over the Pacific and then back onto the beach far below.

Sublime Point ***

Visitors wanting to travel directly to Wollongong should drive down the Southern Freeway. An impressive panorama is offered at Sublime Point, a spectacular lookout from which you can see most of the upper Illawarra, including the whole of the city of Wollongong.

WOLLONGONG **

Wollongong is a great place to go for a day out. It offers the traveller excellent beaches and ideal fishing spots. The city's Botanic Gardens are cool and beautiful. Its history, particularly its coal mining history, is fascinating. The port and Wollongong Harbour are interesting places to visit.

There are a number of ways of entering central Wollongong. If you want a second panoramic view, turn right towards Appin and follow the signs to **Mount Keira**. Drive along Queen Elizabeth Drive to the **Mount Keira Lookout** which offers views of the city with Wollongong University and the Botanic Gardens directly below. It is possible to continue down Mount Keira Road, through the interesting old mining village of Mount Keira, across the Southern Freeway and directly into Crown Street, Wollongong's main street.

Travellers who decide to bypass Mount Keira Lookout and continue down Mount Ousley can turn off the freeway and follow the signs to the university. Drive past the university and you will come to the Botanic Gardens.

Wollongong Botanic Gardens **
Wollongong is justifiably proud of its **Botanic Gardens**. In a little over 20 years the city has managed to establish an impressive collection of indigenous bushes and trees. The small lakes, walkways and pleasant shady areas make the gardens an ideal place for a picnic. People interested in architecture should walk up the hill to **Gleniffer Brae**; the chimneys (fascinating examples of the bricklayer's art) alone are worth the walk.

North Wollongong Beach **
From the Botanic Gardens make your way across to **North Wollongong Beach**, which equals anything in Sydney. The Novotel is a luxury hotel with five-star eating and views across the beach. North of the hotel is a delightful, Mediterranean-style restaurant, **The Lagoon**, located on the lagoon behind the beach. Between Northbeach and The Lagoon is **Stuart Park**, a well-maintained council park with excellent barbecue and picnic facilities.

Below: *Wollongong has a number of excellent beaches. By far the most popular is North Beach, within easy walking distance of the city centre and with excellent restaurants nearby.*

Wollongong Harbour **
South of North Beach is Wollongong's famous harbour. Modest, and with a small fishing fleet, it was once the centre of all activity in the Illawarra. The reason for its early importance is that there are few natural harbours on the coast.

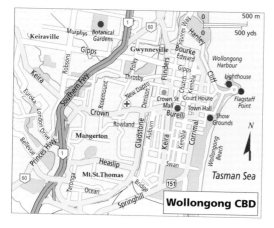

Wollongong CBD

Port Kembla ★

Wollongong's strength is its industry. It is worth driving south to the **Port Kembla Coal Terminal** to see the giant reclaimers scooping up coal, and the conveyor belts shifting mountains of coal to the ships waiting in the harbour to carry it to the power stations and steel mills of Asia, Europe and North America.

From the southernmost points of the breakwater it is possible to get an idea of the size of the harbour and the scale of BHP's huge steel mill. The mill is, however, not open to the public. Where else is there a steel mill only metres away from surfers, fishermen, and people in sailing and power boats?

Crown Street ★

From Port Kembla, turn back to Wollongong. **Crown Street** is Wollongong's main thoroughfare. It is a mixture of a modern shopping mall and a number of interesting

Below: *Now a peaceful boat harbour for private vessels and the local fishing fleet, Wollongong Harbour was once the centre of the region's coal-loading activities. Barges moored in the harbour were loaded with coal, and then made the short journey north to Sydney.*

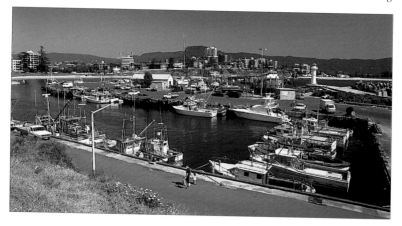

historic buildings. Apart from window shopping and eating at the cafés and restaurants in the mall, it is worthwhile visiting the **Wollongong City Tourist Information Centre** at 87 Crown Street which has walking maps for a self-guided tour of historic Wollongong. The tour includes the Court House, built in 1884 and, most importantly, St Michael's Church of England, built in 1859 and standing on top of the hill in Church Street.

THE SOUTHERN HIGHLANDS
Bowral **

To the southwest of Sydney lie the historic towns of Bowral and Berrima. Located 126km (80 miles) from Sydney the **Bowral** district was first explored in 1798. The first settlement was by Lieutenant John Oxley who moved into the area in 1815 and Dr. Charles Throsby who arrived two years later. In 1825 Oxley took possession of 2000ha (5000 acres) of land, part of which was a large rocky outcrop known as Mt Gibraltar on 'The Gib' and called 'Bowrel' (meaning 'high') by the local Aborigines. An obvious starting point when visiting the town is to travel up to 'The Gib' via Oxley Drive off Mittagong Road. It offers superb views of both Bowral and Mittagong from a road that winds through attractive bushland.

In the 1920s the area became a popular retreat from the summer heat of Sydney. Families would stay at guesthouses and hotels such as **Craigieburn** (before the town centre, turn right off Mittagong Road and go under the railway line) where golf and tennis were popular leisure activities. If you want to experience what this rather glamorous Edwardian lifestyle was like, then a visit to Craigieburn is a must. The hotel has not been modernized and still has a certain 'bygone charm' with formal dining rooms, gracious lounge rooms and wide verandahs. The gardens are delightful.

Above: *Wollongong is the third largest city in New South Wales. Its centre is characterized by Crown Street Mall, surrounded by arcades, shops and department stores.*

TOP ATTRACTIONS OF THE SOUTHERN HIGHLANDS

*** Berrima: a superbly preserved 19th-century town which has remained relatively untouched.
** Milton Park: a truly luxurious hotel and a fascinating insight into the Highland retreats of wealthy Sydneysiders in the 1920s.
** Bradman Museum: a suitable monument to Australia's greatest sportsman.

Above: *The Southern Highlands are noted for their elegant towns and the peaceful countryside.*

Tulip Time Festival ★★

Bowral's current tourist appeal is based on its famous Tulip Time Festival held during the September school holidays. The festival offers visitors profuse floral displays and a rare opportunity to wander the sumptuous, if distinctively English, gardens of some of the town's larger private homes. The centrepiece of the festival is **Corbett Gardens** which are specially prepared for the thousands of visitors who arrive to admire the blooms. Nearby is **St Jude's Church of England** with its gracious rectory, completed in 1880 at a cost of £1,169. The northeast corner of Boolwey Street and Bong Bong Street was the site of the town's first home – a log cabin owned by an Aborigine named Adam.

South Coast

Blue Mountains National Park
Warragamba
Liverpool
Bankstown
SYDNEY
Werombi
89
Sutherland
Camden
Campbelltown
Lake Burragorang
The Oaks
31
Heathcote N.P.
Waterfall
The Royal N.P.
Oakdale
Picton
Douglas Park
Appin
Stanwell Park
Scarborough
Tahmoor
Wilton
Coledale
Buxton
89
Thirroul
Woonona
Tasman
Hilltop
Bargo
60
Corrimal
Sea
Colo Vale
Wollongong
Unanderra
Berrima
Mittagong
Port Kembla
31
Bowral
Macquarie Pass N.P.
Lake Illawarra
115
Windang
N
Moss Vale
Robertson
48
Warilla
Shellharbour
Jamberoo
Bundanoon
Minnamurra
0   15 km
Kangaroo Valley
Kiama
Morton National Park
Berry
Gerringong
0   10 miles

Bradman Museum ★★

Boolwey Street leads to Bradman Oval, home of the recently completed Bradman Museum – a must for all cricket lovers and admirers of one of the country's top sport stars.

Donald Bradman arrived in Bowral as a child, scored a century for the local cricket club at the age of 12, and lived for three years at 20 Glebe Road, opposite the oval. The Bradman Museum, which is located in the park next to the oval, has a display of Bradman memorabilia. It was opened by Bradman in 1989.

Milton Park ★★

Six kilometres (4 miles) out of Bowral on the road to Robertson is Milton Park, a huge stately home and now a fashionable hotel, built in 1910 by Anthony Hordern, a well-known Sydney department store owner. Although the building has been modernized with fashionable pastel hues and modern designer furniture, the gardens are still sumptuous and immaculately kept. The original Garden Room, now the restaurant, allows the visitor a hint of past genteel luxury and offers a splendid, relaxing view.

Berrima ★★★

Returning to Bowral, the visitor can cross the railway line near the station, turn left and follow a road which winds across country to Berrima, a town which is a feast of historic riches. The *Two Foot Tour of Historic Berrima*, a single sheet suggesting places to inspect, lists no fewer than 23 buildings of historic significance. Berrima is a small village. Most of its historic buildings are located in half a dozen streets around what was once the central market place.

EATING IN THE SOUTHERN HIGHLANDS

There are a number of good restaurants in the Southern Highlands. Notable are:
• **Milton Park**, Horderns Rd, Bowral, tel: (048) 61-1522. Quality French cuisine in a sophisticated atmosphere.
• **The Catch**, Bong Bong St, Bowral, tel: (048) 62-2677. Excellent seafood restaurant
• **Thonburi**, Bowral Road, Mittagong, tel: (048) 72-1511. Classy Thai restaurant.

Left: *Bowral in the Southern Highlands is where the famous Australian cricketer Don Bradman grew up.*

Above: *Berrima is one of the best preserved historic towns in New South Wales, with buildings dating from the early 19th century.*

**CLIMATE OF THE
SOUTHERN HIGHLANDS**

The Southern Highlands are significantly colder than Sydney. They were used as a retreat from Sydney's summer humidity in the 1920s. The air is fresh and crisp. There are clear seasonal variations, with autumn being suitably spectacular and snow often falling in winter – although it is light and rarely settles. Expect the Southern Highlands to be up to 5°C (9°F) colder than Sydney.

The town was surveyed in 1832. Two years later, convicts started cutting stone from the banks of the Wingecarribee River and the building of the gaol commenced. By 1838 the Court House had been completed and by the 1840s the town, with its large number of hotels and inns, was looking as though it would develop into a major regional centre.

The decision to move the district court to Goulburn in 1850 and the bypassing of the town by the railway in the 1860s ensured that the development of the town abruptly stopped. The result was, at first, a prosperous town which began to die (by 1914 the population was only 80 people) and then began to grow as a tourist attraction.

Today the town is a marvellous example of a relatively unchanged Georgian colonial township. It is hardly surprising that the whole town has been listed by the National Trust. The range of buildings is remarkable. Undoubtedly the most significant are the **Gaol** and **Court House** which stand at the centre of the town. It is worth noting that the gaol is the oldest Australian gaol still standing (it is still in use) and the **Surveyor-General Inn** is the oldest continuously licensed premises on mainland Australia.

No visit to the gaol is complete without going around the side and marvelling at the Bull's Head Fountain. Made of iron, it was added to the gaol in 1877. The idea was that runoff from the gaol's roof would pour from the bull's mouth into the horse's drinking trough below.

The inns still standing in Berrima have changed their function over the years. Only the Surveyor-General Inn still operates as a hotel. The others – **Taylor's Crown Inn** and the **Colonial Inn** – have been turned into restaurants and gift shops. They are all worth visiting.

Berrima is a town designed for tourists and travellers. You can picnic in the park, eat in a variety of restaurants, coffee lounges and tearooms and shop till you drop. There is something for everyone.

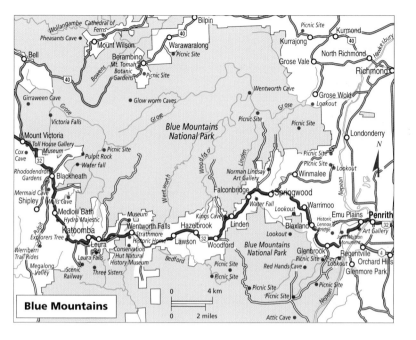

Blue Mountains

THE BLUE MOUNTAINS AND SURROUNDS
Blue Mountains ★★★

Without doubt, the most spectacular experience within easy reach of Sydney is that offered by the Blue Mountains. On a clear day it is easy from high vantage points near the city to see the mountains touched with that distinctive smoky blue which rises, shimmering, from the dense stands of eucalypts.

The early explorers thought that all they had to do was follow a river to its source, climb the valley and cross over the mountains. However, every time they followed a river upstream they came not to an ever-steepening valley or gorge but to a waterfall which fell hundreds of metres over a sheer, unclimbable cliff. The mountains were not crossed until 1813. By the 1880s they had become a major tourist attraction and a kind of Australian 'hill station' where people could escape the summer humidity of Sydney.

**TOP ATTRACTIONS
OF THE BLUE MOUNTAINS**

Katoomba is the main tourist attraction with its spectacular views across the Grose and Jamison valleys. Visitors make special visits to:
★★★ Three Sisters: on the edge of the Jamison Valley.
★★★ Skyway: scenic railway.
★★★ The waterfalls at **Govett's Leap** are dramatic and beautiful.
★★★ Jenolan Caves: a day trip from Sydney. Excellent caves and marvellous scenery.
★★ Norman Lindsay's home: beautiful Springwood cottage in delightful grounds. Home of one of Australia's most admired artists.

Above: *In the 1920s and 1930s people caught the train from Sydney to stay in the elegant Hydro Majestic Hotel at Medlow Bath in the Blue Mountains. Today the hotel still stands although the 'bright young things' have long departed.*

BLUE MOUNTAINS CLIMATE

The Blue Mountains were used as a retreat from the city's summer humidity by 'polite' society in the 1920s. Temperatures in the mountains vary considerably, with Richmond being particularly cold (often as cold as Canberra in winter) but, as a general principal, the weather gets colder the further into the mountains you move. It is quite common for Katoomba, Mount Victoria and Blackheath to experience light snow in winter. Glenbrook can also be hot in summer.

Today the Blue Mountains have a special charm. The air is bracing – in fact, it is quite common for **Katoomba** at 1017m (3337ft) above sea level to have snow in winter. In the 1920s and 1930s it was *the* place for a holiday, and hotels like **The Carrington** at Katoomba, Cooper's **Grand Hotel** and the **Hydro Majestic** at **Medlow Bath** gained reputations as places for a risqué weekend away from the prying eyes and gossiping tongues of Sydney society.

Sights to See

The views offered in the Blue Mountains, particularly from Katoomba, are awe-inspiring. The most striking and impressive formations – Govett's Leap, the Three Sisters, the Jenolan Caves – are beautiful beyond description. The smudgy blueness of the mountains, the gleeming snows of winter, the changing seasons, the invigorating mountain air, and the delightful little villages which are dotted along the railway line, all make this a special area.

If you want to spend only a day, then it would be wise to focus your attentions on the Norman Lindsay Gallery and Museum at Springwood, the Sublime Point Lookout and the quaint shopping centre at Leura, and the Paragon Cafe, Three Sisters Lookout, Skyway and Scenic Railway at Katoomba.

Glenbrook

Located 64km (40 miles) from Sydney, **Glenbrook** is an obvious starting point to the mountains proper because on the Great Western Highway there is an excellent **Tourist Information Centre** (tel: (047) 39-6266), providing travellers with bushwalking maps and brochures as well as details of how to get to the main sights.

Springwood *

Springwood, 74km (46 miles) from Sydney, is a genuinely charming and attractive township which first came to prominence when the Blue Mountains became a fashionable resort in the 1880s. For bushwalkers, one of the attractions is the **Fairy Dell** which is located no more than 10 minutes from the railway station. The ferns, native plants and peaceful bush settings are delightful.

Norman Lindsay's House **

Between Springwood and **Faulconbridge** is one of the mountains' most famous attractions – the painter Norman Lindsay's house, which has been converted into a gallery and museum including the painter's studio. It is clearly signposted from the highway. Lindsay moved to the mountains in 1911 and made the house a centre for artists and writers. Not surprisingly, it became a popular retreat.

Below: *One of Katoomba's most spectacular attractions is the Skyway which runs across one of the box canyons near the town. It can be a hair-raising experience as passengers can actually see the valley below between the boards at the bottom of the carriage.*

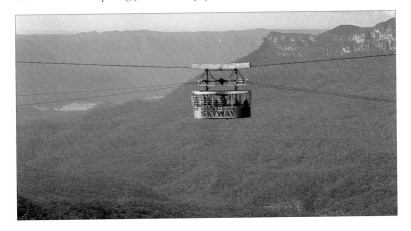

The house and gardens are now owned by the National Trust, which has preserved the statues in the gardens (the gardens are particularly beautiful when the wisteria is in full bloom) and produced an excellent display of Lindsay's art. Lindsay was a prodigious and highly original talent. His skills ranged from cartoons and paintings (oils and watercolours) to statues, model ship building, etchings, pen and pencil drawings, novel and children's fiction writing, book illustration, furniture and pottery decoration.

Leura ***

Beyond Faulconbridge lies **Leura**. To the east of the town is the route to the **Sublime Point Lookout**, regarded by many as the finest of all the lookouts in the Blue Mountains. **Everglades**, a National Trust property in Leura, has 5ha (12 acres) of gardens which mix native bushland with displays of bluebells, daffodils, rhododendrons and azaleas.

But it is the Mall and Cliff Drive which hold most appeal to visitors. A walk down The Mall, with its vast number of tea houses, gift shops, restaurants and cafés, is like nothing else in the Blue Mountains.

A brochure, *Walking Tracks in the Leura Area*, published by the National Parks and Wildlife Service includes a detailed contour map and describes five walks in the area.

The **Cliff Drive** between Leura and Katoomba is a highlight of any visit to the area. The views across the Megalong and Jamison valleys, the different angles on the **Three Sisters**, the **Ruined Castle** and **Mount Solitary**, the variety of excellent picnic spots and the range of lookouts make this a must for anyone wanting to experience the beauty of the area.

Below: *The Blue Mountains' most famous landmark is the Three Sisters, a rocky outcrop near Katoomba. Endlessly photographed, and climbed, they symbolise the beauty and ruggedness of the area.*

Left: *A number of waterfalls tumble from the Blue Mountains over the cliffs into the valleys, the most beautiful being the Wentworth Falls.*

Katoomba ★★★

Katoomba is the true heart of the Blue Mountains. A visit should start at **Echo Point**. It offers superb views, and the **Blue Mountains Tourist Centre** will provide all the maps and information you may need.

Echo Point offers exceptional views of the Three Sisters, Mount Solitary, the Ruined Castle and the Jamison Valley. Be sure to see the Three Sisters, Katoomba Falls and Leura Cascades floodlit at night.

You can cross the Jamison Valley in the **Katoomba Scenic Skyway**. This is not for the faint-hearted. The aerial cable car floats 275m (900ft) above the valley floor and looks over the Katoomba Falls and Orphan Rock. The first horizontal passenger-carrying ropeway in the Southern Hemisphere, it was completed in 1958.

Nearby is the **Scenic Railway**, dropping 230m (750ft) into the Jamison Valley. Built in the 1880s to bring coal from the valley to the clifftop, and to take miners down, it is claimed to be the steepest railway in the world.

A walk down Katoomba Street will take the visitor to the town's other famous attraction, **The Paragon Café**, now listed by the National Trust because of its superb 1930s art deco interior. The Paragon offers excellent afternoon tea and the fare includes delicious handmade chocolates.

HENRY PARKES

On the road between Springwood and Faulconbridge is the Prime Ministers' Avenue of Oaks in Jackson Park. Joseph Jackson, a NSW MP, gave the park to the local council in 1933 with the explicit intention of having every Australian Prime Minister, or a nearest surviving relative, plant an oak tree. Jackson was a huge admirer of Henry Parkes and believed that his Avenue of Oaks was a suitable monument to the man most responsible for the federation of the Australian states. Parkes moved to Faulconbridge in 1877. It is said that the original railway platform at Faulconbridge was specifically built to serve his residence, which was known as Faulconbridge House.

Right: *One of the major tourist attractions in the Blue Mountains is the home of the Australian artist Norman Lindsay in Springwood. The gardens have a number of Lindsay's sensuous statues.*

Medlow Bath *

The small village of **Medlow Bath** is 6km (4 miles) west of Katoomba. Its fame relies on the **Hydro Majestic** hotel which, in keeping with the medicinal qualities of the mountains, was built as a 'hydropathic establishment' in the late 19th century by the Sydney businessman Mark Foy. Originally conceived as a health resort, Foy established the hotel's reputation by instituting a strict regime of therapies. He even had fresh produce brought up from the Megalong Valley on a specially installed flying fox. Today the Hydro Majestic is a hotel where you can enjoy afternoon tea with spectacular views.

Blackheath **

Five kilometres (3 miles) beyond Medlow Bath is **Blackheath**, a town famous for its superb rhododendron displays, the magnificent northerly views at **Govett's Leap**, the bushwalks around the edges of the Grose Valley and its range of expensive and luxurious guest houses.

It would seem, if you arrive in season, that everyone in Blackheath plants rhododendrons in their garden. For the serious admirer, the **Rhododendron Garden** in Bacchante Street (open 09:00–17:00 daily) has established a careful harmony between native flora and the rhododendron. There are more than 1500 rhododendrons in the gardens.

WEST OF THE BLUE MOUNTAINS
Jenolan Caves ★★★

At the northern end of the Kanangra Boyd National Park,
the most popular and accessible cave complex within easy
reach of Sydney. The **Jenolan Caves** are located 164km
(100 miles) from Sydney in a valley on the far side of the
Great Dividing Range. It is sensible to take at least a day to
visit the caves complex.

After winding down a hill, the road comes out on a
river with an incredibly blue pond. Straight ahead is the
Grand Arch of the main cave which visitors have to drive
through before emerging just below **Caves House**. The
Grand Arch is the largest open cave in Australia. It is 24m
(80ft) high, 55m (180ft) wide and 127 (400ft) long. It is an
extraordinary introduction to the caves.

There are 22 major caves in the Jenolan system. Of
these, nine – the Imperial, Chifley, Jubilee, Lucas,
Skeleton, River, Orient, Temple of Baal and Ribbon – are
'dark caves' opened for guided inspection. The caves feature the range of formations with symbolic names like
'Gem of the West', 'Gabriel's Wing', 'Lot's Wife' and the
'Bishop and Three Sisters'.

Beyond the caves there are also excellent bushwalks in
the area. Jenolan is a 2430ha (6000 acres) flora and fauna
sanctuary and walkers in
the area are likely to see
lyrebirds, wallabies, possums, kangaroos and, if
they are lucky, wombats.

It would be easy to
spend a few days at the
hotel, which has a delightful old-world charm and
offers the visitor excellent
opportunities to experi-
ence a rich and unusual
bush experience. For
details of accommodation,
contact **Jenolan Caves
House**, tel: (063) 59-3304.

Below: *Jenolan Caves
lie beyond the Blue
Mountains. A fine collec-
tion of interesting limestone
caves, they are nestled in a
valley far removed from
towns and urban develop-
ment. They are a very full
daytrip from Sydney.*

WINDSOR **

Historic Windsor, about 57km (35 miles) northwest of Sydney, was the third European settlement in Australia after Sydney Cove and Parramatta. The town's highlights include St Matthews Church, the Court House, Tebbutt's observatories, the graveyard at the church, and the numerous buildings dating back to the early 19th century.

Above: *Windsor, one of the five towns built by Governor Macquarie, lies on the Hawkesbury River plains to the west of the city centre. The township has a number of fine 19th-century buildings, a historic observatory and a fascinating cemetery.*

Thompson Square **

The **Hawkesbury Museum and Tourist Centre**, located in Thompson Square, has a wide range of information including maps and descriptive walks. The museum's displays include Aboriginal artefacts, European settlement of the area from earliest times, development of the town after 1810 and the river economy of the 19th century. The museum was built in the 1820s and used as an inn before becoming the office of *The Australian* newspaper from 1871 to 1899. The centre is open 10:00–16:00 daily.

Thompson Square is a good place to start any walk around Windsor. It is a fine example of the orderliness Macquarie brought to a temporary, rather ramshackle, society. A westward route along George Street passes the **Macquarie Arms Hotel**, built in 1815 and, apart from the period between 1840 and 1874, used continuously as a hotel. On the museum side of the hotel there is a mark on the wall indicating the level reached by the floods of 1867. Further along the street are the old **CBC Bank**, the **Windsor Post Office** and **Mrs Copes Cottage**.

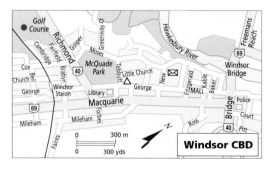

Windsor CBD

St Matthew's Anglican Church **

The town's highlight is **St Matthew's**, known affectionately as the 'Cathedral of the Hawkesbury'. It is widely acknowledged as one of the best works of the convict architect, Francis Greenway, and was built by convicts between 1817 and 1820. The huge square tower can be seen from some distance away.

The church's gravestones provide a fascinating insight into the early life of the town. No gravestone is more interesting than that of Andrew Thompson, who died in 1810. Thompson, after whom Thompson Square was named, was a convict who arrived in Australia in 1792 after being transported for 14 years for stealing cloth worth £10. He subsequently became the first emancipist appointed as a magistrate and was the first person buried in the graveyard at St Matthew's.

Windsor Court House *

Returning towards Sydney on Macquarie Street, just after the turn towards the bridge over South Creek, is Court Street on the left. On the corner of Court Street and Pitt Street is the **Windsor Court House**, another fine building designed by Francis Greenway. It was built in 1822, and after considerable alteration, was restored to its former glory in 1960. It has warm sandstock bricks and stone lintels and an excellent contemporary portrait of Lachlan Macquarie.

John Tebbutt Observatory **

Continue on down Court/North Street and turn right into Palmer Street to **John Tebbutt Observatory**. Tebbutt, a gentleman farmer and talented amateur astronomer, was born in Windsor in 1834. In 1845 his father built the house in Palmer Street which John inherited in 1870. John built both a wooden and brick observatory which still stand, and the house is still owned by the Tebbutt family. Tebbutt achieved particular fame in 1984 when it was decided to include his portrait on the $100 note. The observatories are open for inspection. For more information, tel: (02) 9627-2225 or (047) 77-3120.

WINDSOR'S EARLY HISTORY

Governor Macquarie was a great builder and dreamer. He established the five Macquarie towns in the Hawkesbury Valley – Windsor, Richmond, Castlereagh, Wilberforce and Pitt Town. Of all these towns, it is Windsor which stands as a monument to Macquarie. Of course, Windsor pre-dates Macquarie. As early as 1789 Governor Phillip had explored the district and, although it was considered isolated, the colony's need for food and the richness of the alluvial Hawkesbury river flats ensured that settlement occurred.

Above: *To the north of Sydney, the Hawkesbury River basin separates the city from the Central Coast. It is a popular place for boating with excellent mooring facilities at Coal and Candle Creek. At the mouth of the river is the impressive Lion Island.*

KU-RING-GAI CHASE NATIONAL PARK **

The Ku-ring-gai Chase National Park is the city's northerly barrier. Suburban development reaches to the borders of the park then leaps across the **Hawkesbury River** and **Broken Bay** to start again on the Central Coast.

The Ku-ring-gai Chase National Park is a true escape from the city. It is close and yet, when you start wandering along the bush tracks or start clambering around the rocky headlands and small beaches, you suddenly feel as though you are in a bushland which hasn't changed for thousands of years.

Covering 14,658ha (36,200 acres) and about 24km (15 miles) from the centre of Sydney, the **Ku-ring-gai Chase National Park** is located on the sandstones and shales of the Sydney basin. The geological history of the park is that about 200 million years ago the whole area was covered by sea and sand. Fifty million years later the rocks which had been formed by these deep deposits of sand were uplifted and, as they rose, the creeks and rivers running to the ocean, cut deep valleys. When the ice melted after the last ice age (around 6000 years ago) the valleys were drowned, forming Broken Bay and the subsidiary valley systems of **Pittwater**, **Coal and Candle Creek**, **Smith's Creek**, **Cowan Creek** and **Berowra Waters**.

The result is Sydney sandstone covered by sandy soils which produce a kind of heathland on the plateau and eucalypts in the valleys. It seems extraordinary, given the poorness of the soils, but Ku-ring-gai Chase has over 900 native species of flora and a surprising diversity of fauna.

Flora and Fauna

The range of eucalypts – the Sydney red gum and scribbly gum are in abundance, the angophoras, the varieties of coastal banksia, the wattles and the wildflower displays make any walk through the park a discovery. In the gullies the keen bushwalker will find coachwood, water gums and turpentine.

The winter and spring wildflower displays in the park are truly magnificent. The dramatic red of the waratah is matched by purple and pink boronias, yellow pea flowers, and the pink and white heath make it a native flower wonderland. There are few places on the eastern coast, and particularly so close to Sydney, where such displays are so readily accessible.

The Dhurag people lived in the area before European settlement and the park is still the most abundant source of the local Aboriginal art and culture in the Sydney basin.

Bobbin Head **

To gain access to **Bobbin Head** visitors can drive up the Pacific Highway and beyond Hornsby, at Mt Colah, take Ku-ring-gai Chase Road; or drive down Bobbin Head Road which runs off the Pacific Highway near Pymble.

Bobbin Head is the park's most developed area, with the Halvorsen Boat Sheds offering cruisers for hire. There is a large picnic area with extensive parking and good barbecue facilities.

Visitors interested in the park's diverse fauna and flora will find the **Kalkari Visitors Centre** (1.5km/ 1 mile, west of Bobbin Head on the Ku-ring-gai Chase Road) an ideal starting point. The centre has displays which detail the flora and fauna. It also has maps and information for bushwalkers. The walks are, in many instances, defined by coloured and numbered signs.

Above: *Houseboats can be hired at the Brooklyn Marina on the Hawkesbury River and this is a wonderful way to experience the Ku-ring-gai Chase National Park.*

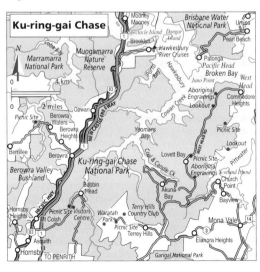

If you enter the park from Bobbin Head Road you will pass Lady Davidson Rehabilitation Hospital – a hospital for victims of the two world wars. It is a comment on the life of these men and women that just within the gates of the National Park is a **Sphinx War Memorial** (turn right after entering the park) which was carved out of the Hawkesbury sandstone by diggers recuperating at the hospital. The Sphinx is a strange memento of the fact that so many Anzacs stopped in Egypt before being shipped across the Mediterranean to Gallipoli.

Near the Sphinx War Memorial is the start of the **Bobbin Head Track** which winds through the bush to the wharves at Bobbin Head. The Sphinx Track, which starts behind the War Memorial, goes down to Cowan Creek and follows it to Bobbin Head.

Coal and Candle Creek **

The other main entrance to the Ku-ring-gai Chase National Park is via Terrey Hills on Mona Vale Road. This entrance offers the visitor a round trip to **Coal and Candle Creek** or a trip out to West Head. The Coal and Candle Creek journey passes through bushland before tumbling down to the edges of Broken Bay.

West Head ***

A favourite sightseeing location in the Ku-ring-gai Chase National Park is the lookout at West Head, sometimes called **Commodore Heights**. This superb view of the mouth of the drowned **Hawkesbury River** has views across to **Lion Island** (so named because from various angles it looks like a crouching lion), to **Patonga** and to the isthmus of sand which separates Palm Beach from the **Barrenjoey** headland. There can be few views in the Sydney area to compare with the wonderful diversity and beauty of this view. It is possible from this point to walk down to **Pittwater** (the beaches below are ideal locations for picnics), and for those who are keen it is possible to walk around to **The Basin** (a marvellous expanse of water protected from Pittwater by a narrow channel) and catch the ferry across to **Palm Beach**.

THE CENTRAL COAST **

In the 1940s and 1950s the Central Coast became the premier commuter zone for people wanting to live outside the Sydney metropolitan area. Initial development of the area had been slow. Broken Bay was isolated, and the only easy access to Sydney was by boat, either across to Barrenjoey or around the coast to Sydney Harbour. A major change occurred in 1889 when the Hawkesbury Bridge linked Brisbane Water to Sydney. This opened up the area, but the two major post-war events – the construction of the Sydney–Newcastle freeway to Calga and the electrification of the railway line – converted this quiet backwater into a desirable beach resort-commuter belt.

Old Sydney Town **

The starting point for any visit to the Brisbane Water area is **Old Sydney Town**, described by its publicity as follows: 'This is where it all began. A faithful recreation of Australia's birthplace, as it was nearly 200 years ago. There are the buildings – the Windmill, the Church, the Gaol, the Tradespeople's Cottages with their thatched or shingled roofs, Lieutenant Dawe's Observatory. They're all here painstakingly and authentically recreated . . . It is in fact a living museum, inhabited by costumed characters living out the lives of those colourful, early settlers.'

Below: *In the numerous inlets and bays which are part of Broken Bay (the mouth of the Hawkesbury River) there are marinas and mooring facilities. At Akuna Bay the marina offers mooring to sailors from all over the world.*

Above: *Sunrise at the entrance to Broken Bay captures the beauty of the area surrounding Barrenjoey Lighthouse.*

Old Sydney Town is an outstanding re-creation. The 'actors' who live out the life of the settlers are convincing and the situations which unfold on the streets, especially the popular whippings (which says something about our unchanging attitude to violence), are well staged. It is an excellent introduction to the history of the Sydney basin and the difficulties experienced by the first Europeans.

Gosford and Environs

Past Old Sydney Town is **Gosford,** a modern city with shopping arcades and supermarkets, and a fast electric train service to Sydney. It is the centre of the rapidly growing urban area on this part of the coast. Beyond the city is **Avoca Beach**, a popular resort which attracts people from all over Sydney. Avoca is an ideal place for a picnic, a surf or a run along the beach.

TOP ATTRACTIONS OF THE CENTRAL COAST

*** **Brisbane Waters National Park:** one of the best displays of Aboriginal artwork within the Sydney area.
** **Old Sydney Town:** an excellent re-creation of life in Sydney at the beginning of the 19th century. A popular tourist attraction.
** **Bouddi National Park:** an untouched coastal wilderness with superb views down to Sydney.

Left: *A recreation of Sydney in the early 19th century, Old Sydney Town is a popular attraction a few kilometres west of Gosford on the Central Coast. Visitors are treated to re-enactments including coach rides and public whippings.*
Below: *The beaches on the northern shore of Broken Bay offer a peacefulness which is often absent from the beaches closer to Sydney. Patonga has been a quiet retreat from city life for most of this century.*

From Avoca turning towards Kincumber there is a **Scenic Drive** which is a circular route through the **Bouddi National Park**, a small wilderness area of 1148ha (2800 acres) ideal for bushwalking, surfing and picnicking. The views it offers, down the coast to the **Barrenjoey Lighthouse** at Palm Beach, and far beyond to central Sydney, are extraordinary. Bouddi National Park, which includes 283ha (700 acres) of offshore marine lands, is the first National Park in New South Wales to include a marine component. It features coastal scenery of great beauty, spectacular cliffs, and a variety of walks to the isolated and frequently windswept beaches, through rich coastal heathlands and, in some instances, rainforest.

Drive across the **Rip Bridge** and head to **Pearl Beach**, a retreat for the wealthy. This is a place which has a 'very civilized' shopping centre offering outdoor cafés, designer labels and an air of sophistication in the middle of the bush. It is charmingly incongruous to see such urbanity next to a quiet beach and set in stands of gum trees.

Near Pearl Beach, but further inland, is **Woy Woy**. Although smaller than Gosford, Woy Woy is the other major settlement in the area. Its modern malls and supermarkets, sprawling suburban development, and queues of commuters attest to the changes that have occurred on the Central Coast.

From Pearl Beach to Woy Woy the road passes through the southeastern corner of the **Brisbane Water National Park**. This substantial 8242ha (20,400 acres) park is characterized by rugged sandstone, open eucalypt woodlands and small pockets of temperate rainforest.

The greatest attraction is the Bulgandry Aboriginal engraving site. The engravings at Bulgandry are some of the best in the Sydney area. The timber walkways give excellent access to the site. If you are walking in the park, it is quite possible to come across other engravings – it is estimated that there are hundreds in the park – and it is important not to touch them.

Below: *Sun-kissed Terrigal Beach on the Central Coast.*

Located between Sydney and New-castle, the area around **Tuggerah Lake** is one of the best holiday destinations in New South Wales. With a population of about 100,000 (which doubles in summer time) it boasts 82km² (32 sq miles) of protected water – in Lake Munmorah, Lake Budgewoi and Tuggerah Lake – and 121km (75 miles) of lake shoreline.

The largest local industry is tourism, which relies on spectacular ocean beaches for swimming, surfing and sailing, wildlife sanctuaries sheltering unique fauna and flora, walking trails through age-old red gum reserves or in the spectacular Watagan Mountain forest, the pleasures of boating on tranquil lakes or the many diversions (waterslides, art galleries, Sunday markets, potteries, sporting facilities) offered by townships such as Wyong, The Entrance and Toukley as its central selling point to tourists and visitors.

Above: *The Entrance, on the Central Coast, is a thriving holiday town offering both surfing and the quieter waters of the nearby lakes.* **Overleaf:** *Darling Harbour.*

A sensible starting point is the Tuggerah Lakes Tourist Association in Marine Parade at **The Entrance**. The *Tuggerah Lakes Information Guide* provides detailed listings of picnic and barbecue facilities, maps and other information. The Association arranges tours of the **Norah Head Lighthouse** and provides information about the variety of activities around the lakes – everything from visiting Vales Point Power Station to cruising on Lake Macquarie.

The Entrance is geared to holiday activities. At 15:30, near the children's playground in the Memorial Park, there is an organized pelican feeding. At the southern end of the 8km (5 miles) long **Tuggerah Beach** is The Entrance rock pool. Then there's the Aqua Slide, an ideal way of cooling off and having fun on a hot summer day, cruises on the lake, the Wonders of the Sea (a display of corals and shells), and the usual sports like squash and tennis.

There is no doubt that the appeal of the Central Coast does not lie alone in its history. It is a huge fun park. The task for the visitor is simply to choose from the vast number of activities offered in the area to relax and enjoy themselves – which isn't hard.

BELLBIRDS NEAR GOSFORD

The road to Gosford is famous for its bellbirds. The poem 'Bellbirds' is known to generations of Australian schoolchildren who learned the lines:
*'By channels of coolness
the echoes are calling,
And down the dim gorges
I hear the creek falling;
It lives in the mountain
where moss and the sedges
Touch with their beauty the
banks and the ledges.
Through breaks of the
cedar and sycamore bowers
Struggles the light that
is love to the flowers;
And, softer than slumber
and sweeter than singing,
The notes of the bell-birds
are running and ringing.'*
The poet, Henry Kendall, lived in Gosford between 1873 and 1875.

Sydney at a Glance

Sydney
Sydney has a short spring (**September** to **November**) but it comes alive with new blooms. Parks and gardens are noted for their beautiful azaleas and rhododendron displays. The city of beaches knows how to take full advantage of long summer days (**December** to **February**). It can get hot and sticky, but this rarely lasts long.

South Coast
The South Coast is slightly cooler than Sydney.

Southern Highlands
The best time to visit is in the **spring** and **autumn**. Flowering trees and the Tulip Time Festival, 30 September to 15 October, turn the town into a springtime showcase. Autumn has its own colourful display as the trees change colour. Remember: The Southern Highlands are about 5°C (9°F) colder than Sydney.

Blue Mountains
The mountains offer the visitor activities all year. Winter has the Yulefest, while spring sees the mountains ablaze with colour. The Leura Garden Festival in October and the Rhododendron Festival in November are major attractions. Summer is ideal for bushwalkers, and autumn sees the magnificent turning leaves. The Blue Mountains are 5–7C° (41–45F°) cooler than Sydney. It sometimes snows in winter.

Western Districts
This area has merged with Sydney and has become as much a part of Sydney as the northern beaches and southern suburbs.

Central Coast
The Central Coast is slightly warmer than Sydney. Beach culture thrives. **Summer** is the most popular time of year.

Sydney
Sydney's **Kingsford Smith Airport** has both international and domestic terminals. They are 5km (3 miles) apart and 9km (6 miles) from the city centre. **Airport Express Buses** coloured green and gold operate every 10 minutes from both terminals to well-mapped routes in the city and Kings Cross, with stops at most of the major hotels. There is also the **Kingsford Smith Airport Bus** service which operates half-hourly and will usually do specified drop-offs and pick-ups; tel: (02) 9667-3221. Ring the day before for pick-up service. **Taxis** are plentiful and will take you anywhere. Major **car rental** firms are represented at the airport. Useful **airline** contact numbers are:
Air New Zealand, 5 Elizabeth St, tel: 9957-4388.
Ansett Australia, Oxford Sq, Darlinghurst, tel: 13 1767.
British Airways, 64 Castlereagh St, tel: 9258-3300.

Cathay Pacific, Level 5, 28 O'Connel St, tel: 13 1747.
Japan Airlines, 201 Sussex St, tel: 9283-1111.
KLM Royal Dutch Airlines, 5 Elizabeth St, tel: 9231-6333.
Malaysia Airlines, 388 George St, tel: 13 26 27.
QANTAS, cnr Hunter & Phillip Sts, tel: 9957-0111.
Singapore Airlines, 17 Bridge St, tel: 13 1011.
Thai Airways International, 75–77 Pitt St, tel: 9844-0999.
United Airlines, 10 Barrack St, tel: 13 1777.

South Coast
Train travel is definitely the most economical. A fast electric train runs from Central. A slower train stops at all the stations along the coast. Check the timetables with Cityrail. This is one of the most scenic rail journeys in Australia. The train runs through the famous Royal National Park and along the coastline.

Southern Highlands
Trains stop at all the stations in the Southern Highlands. Check timetables with Cityrail. Two coach companies offer a one-day tour of the Highlands. *See* Tours and Excursions on p. 120. Hire car allows mobility.

Blue Mountains
The train is the cheapest and most interesting way of getting to the Blue Mountains. Check the timetable with Cityrail, tel: 13 1500. Cityrail also runs the

Sydney at a Glance

Blue Mountains Explorer Bus which visits the top attractions. Most coach companies have one-, two- and three-day tours of the mountains, with accommodation generally included.

Western Districts
Most forms of public transport, rail and bus, will get you to Parramatta, Penrith or Windsor.

Central Coast
Gosford is commuter territory. An efficient train service runs from Sydney. Check with Cityrail. Car hire offers some independence. Some tour operators offer one-day tours of the area.

GETTING AROUND

There are three types of public transport in Sydney: buses, trains and ferries. All are clearly marked and signposted. For information on trains and buses, ring **MetroTrips**, tel: (02) 9954-4422. The ferries have their own information line, tel: (02) 9256-4670. Timetables for the three services can be picked up at the information booth at Circular Quay. The **Sydney Explorer**, a tourist bus which operates a continuous loop around the tourist sights of the city, runs every 20 minutes. The stops are marked by green and red signs. **Greyhound** transcontinental buses leave from the **Greyhound Pioneer Coach Terminal**, cnr Oxford & Riley Sts, tel: 13 2030. The subur-

ban trains are both fast and efficient, and are clearly marked and colour coded, while the ferry system is the most pleasant way to get around this harbour city.

Car rental firms are represented at most hotels and are competitive. Sydney has an efficient network of both trains and buses. It is important to understand the basic structure of the two systems.

The **trains** radiate out from **Central Railway Station** which lies at the extreme southern end of the city's central business district. This rail system includes a circuit around the city centre with stops at Town Hall, Wynyard, Circular Quay, Martin Place, St James and Museum stations. The trains to the city's eastern suburbs – including Kings Cross and Bondi Junction, run from Martin Place. The train to the city's North Shore, which runs up the ridge through North Sydney, St Leonards and Chatswood to Hornsby, connects with trains which run to the Central Coast, Newcastle and the Queensland border. Trains from Central Railway Station run to all other parts of the city – to Parramatta, in a loop around both the western and northwestern suburbs to connect with the North Shore line at Hornsby, to the southwest,

to the Blue Mountains in the west and to Wollongong in the south. Central Railway Station is also the departure point for the trains which service the whole of the state of New South Wales and for the Indian Pacific rail service which crosses the continent to Perth.

There are a number of popular areas of Sydney which are only serviced by bus. **Buses** can take visitors to Bondi Beach and all the beaches to the south of Sydney Heads. Buses service the northern beaches, departing from both Wynyard and Manly to make the long journey to Avalon, Newport and Palm Beach. Buses service most of the northern harbourside suburbs – places like Hunters Hill, Mosman, Cremorne and Neutral Bay. These suburbs are also serviced by ferry. For visitors on a budget, trains and buses are a cheap alternative to tours and taxis. For information, tel: 13 1500.

Ferries: It has been said that Sydney's ferries are the best form of public transport in the world. While this may be a little exaggerated, they certainly do offer marvellous views of the harbour for the price of a regular journey. All ferries depart from Circular Quay. The public

Sydney at a Glance

routes include a journey to Watson's Bay (near South Head) which occurs only on weekends; ferry and fast Jet Cat journeys to Manly; regular State Transit ferry services to Mosman, Taronga Park Zoo, Neutral Bay, Cremorne, Balmain, Hunters Hill, Parramatta, Meadowbank, Darling Harbour and McMahons Point; and a private ferry service to Kirribilli, Lavender Bay and McMahons Point. Widely recognized as the two best ferry trips are those to **Taronga Zoo** and **Manly**. The zoo is beautifully located on the slopes overlooking the harbour and beyond it is **Athol Park** which offers delightful walks through bushland. On the trip across to Manly the ferry passes North and South Heads and provides many spectacular views of the harbour. For all information about public transport in Sydney, tel: 13 1500.

WHERE TO STAY

Sydney
Sydney is well serviced by hotels, motels and serviced apartments. The central business district has a large range of accommodation, but don't forget the quieter suburban areas which also offer a wide choice of lodgings. Excellent public transport makes the city centre easy to get to.

LUXURY
Hyde Park Plaza Hotel, College St, tel: (02) 9331-6933, fax: 9331-6022. Luxury hotel located in the city centre with excellent facilities.
Hotel Inter-Continental, Macquarie St, tel: (02) 9230-0200, fax: 9240 1240. This luxury hotel is partly housed in the historic Treasury building (1851) in the centre of the city.
Parkroyal Darling Harbour, Day St, tel: (02) 9261-4444, fax: 9261-8766. Opposite the Darling Harbour complex. Quality hotel; excellent service.
Sydney Regent Hotel, George St, tel: (02) 9238-8000, fax: 9251-2851. Best views in Sydney from this luxury hotel.
Novotel Sydney on Darling Harbour, 100 Murray St, tel: (02) 9934-0000, fax: 9934-0099. Luxury hotel in the heart of the famous Darling Harbour complex.
Harbourside Serviced Apartments, 24 Henry Lawson Ave, McMahons Point, tel: (02) 9963-4300, fax: 9922-7998. Fully serviced apartments on the harbour, seven minutes to the city by ferry.

MID-RANGE
The Cambridge, Riley St, tel: (02) 9212-2111, fax: 9281-1981. Well-located reasonably priced hotel with all facilities.
Hyde Park Inn, 271 Elizabeth St, tel: (02) 9264-6001, fax: 9261-8691. Well-located, comfortable family motel. Easy walk to the city centre.

BUDGET
All Season Harbour Rocks Hotel, Herrington St, tel: (02) 9251-8944, fax: 9251-8900. Medium-sized hotel located in the heart of The Rocks.

YOUTH HOSTELS
Youth Hostels Travel Centre, 422 Kent St, tel: (02) 9261-1111.

South Coast
LUXURY
Novotel Northbeach Hotel, 1–14 Cliff Rd, North Wollongong, tel: (02) 26-3555, fax: 29-1705. The premier resort offering luxury accommodation on the beach.

MID-RANGE
City Pacific Hotel, 112 Burelli St, Wollongong, tel: (042) 29-7444, fax: 28-0552. This boutique-style hotel offers excellent accommodation in the heart of Wollongong.
Boat Harbour Motel, Wilson St, Wollongong, tel: (042) 28-9166, fax: 26-4878. Comfortable family motel opposite the beach.

BUDGET
Golden Pacific North Beach, 16 Pleasant Ave, North Wollongong, tel: (042) 26-3000, fax: 28-3853. Well-located motel offering the usual motel-type accommodation and family units with kitchens.

Sydney at a Glance

Southern Highlands
Luxury
Milton Park, Horderns Rd, Bowral, tel: (048) 61-1522, fax: 61-4716, toll free 008 818 329. Eight hectares (20 acres) of formal gardens surround this beautiful resort.

Berida Manor Country Hotel, 6 David St, Bowral, tel: (048) 61-1177, fax: 61-1219. Centrally located, elegant guesthouse with old-world charm offering comfortable accommodation.

Mid-range
Ivy Tudor Motor Inn, cnr Moss Vale & Links Rds, Bowral, tel: (048) 61-2911. Reasonable prices; close to town centre.

Berrima Bakehouse Motel, cnr Wingecarribee St & Hume Hwy, Berrima, tel: (048) 77-1381, fax: 77-1047. Family motel in the heart of Berrima.

Budget
White Horse Inn, Market Pl, Berrima, tel: (048) 77-1204. Well-located motel.

Blue Mountains
Accommodation in the Blue Mountains ranges from five-star resorts to elegant guesthouses, family motels and cabins. The **Visitors Information Centre** at Glenbrook has a comprehensive list of all the services in the mountains. It offers an accommodation referral service. They will match the visitor up to the price and type of accommodation and make the booking.

Luxury
Lilianfels Blue Mountains Resort, Lilianfels Ave, Katoomba, tel: (047) 80-1200, fax: 80-1300. Resort in picturesque Katoomba with a wide range of activities in complete luxury.

Fairmont Resort, 1 Sublime Point Rd, Leura, tel: (047) 82-5222, fax: 84-1685. A well-established family resort situated on extensive grounds with golf, swimming and tennis facilities.

Leura House, 7 Britain Rd, Leura, tel: (047) 84-2035. Historic home (c1880) converted to an elegant guesthouse.

Mid-range
The Claredon Motor Inn, 68 Lurline Rd, Katoomba, tel: (047) 82-1322. Small, comfortable motel well located in the heart of Katoomba.

Mount Victoria Motor Inn, Station St, Mount Victoria, tel: (047) 87-1320. Family motel well located in this small mountain town.

Norwood Guesthouse, 209 Great Western Hwy, Blackheath, tel: (047) 87-8568. Small historic guesthouse (c1888) with old-style hospitality at an affordable price.

Budget
Echo Point Motor Inn, Echo Point, Katoomba, tel: (047) 82-2088, fax: 82-5546. Comfortable, well-located motel just a few metres from the Three Sisters.

Hotel Imperial, Station St, Mount Victoria, tel: (047) 87-1233. Old hotel with atmosphere and mountain hospitality.

Western Districts
Panthers Resort, Mulgoa Rd, Penrith, tel: (047) 21-7700, fax: 21-8032. Large resort on the Nepean River with motel and cottage accommodation; offers family entertainment.

Parkroyal Parramatta, 30 Phillips St, Parramatta, tel: (02) 9685-0333, fax: 9689-3959. Convenient, luxurious motel.

Radisson Rum Corps Resort, 61 Richmond Rd, Windsor, tel: (045) 77-4222. Excellent motel with every luxury well positioned to explore this village. Like all suburbs of a large city, most restaurants are near the shopping centre.

Central Coast
Luxury
Holiday Inn Crown Plaza, Pine Tree Lane, Terrigal, tel: (043) 84-9111, toll free 008 024 966. On Terrigal beach, this luxury hotel offers the visitor complete service and amenities.

Apollo Country Resort, 871 The Entrance Rd, Wamberal, tel: (043) 85-1555, fax: 85-1476. A well-equipped resort.

Mid-range
El Lago Waters Resort, 41 The Entrance Rd, The Entrance, tel: (043) 32-3955, fax: 32-6188. Family motel opposite Tuggerah Lakes.

Sydney at a Glance

The Palms Motor Inn,
7 Moore St, West Gosford,
tel: (043) 23-1211, fax:(043)
23-4558. Quiet location with
easy access to Gosford.
Villa Sorgenti, Kowara Rd,
West Gosford, tel: (043)
40-1205, fax: 40-2758.
Small resort nestled in the
beautiful Australian bush.

BUDGET
Pinehurst Holiday Villas, 11
The Entrance Rd, The Entrance,
tel: (043) 32-2002. Fully self-
contained lakeside apartments.

Rambler Motor Inn, 73
Pacific Hwy, Gosford West, tel:
(043) 24-6577, fax: 25-1780.
Centrally located hotel.

WHERE TO EAT

Sydney
Every conceivable variety of
food is on offer throughout
the city and its environs.
Restaurants cluster in pockets:
Oxford St from Hyde Park
to Paddington has a large
selection of interesting
ethnic restaurants.
Glebe Point Rd in Glebe
offers over 40 restaurants.
King St in Newtown is the
latest restaurant cluster.
There are several magazines
that cover restaurants. *This
Week in Sydney* is put out
by the NSW Government
Tourist Travel Centre.
Widely recognized as
authoritative is the *Sydney
Morning Herald's Good
Food Guide*, available in

newsagencies and, as a guide
to moderately priced eateries
around town, the *Sydney
Morning Herald Cheap Eats*
guide is highly recommended.
Bayswater Brasserie, Kings
Cross, tel: (02) 9357-2177.
A stylish brasserie with
excellent service.
Doyles on the Beach, Watsons
Bay, tel: (02) 9337-2077. Sea-
food restaurant on the beach
overlooking the harbour.
Harbour Restaurant,
Sydney Opera House, tel: (02)
9250-7191. Dine in complete
style at one of Sydney's most
famous landmarks.
**Imperial Peking
Harbourside Restaurant**,
Circular Quay West, tel:
(02) 9247-7073. Sydney's
most perfectly located
Chinese restaurant looks
across to the Opera House.
John Cadman, No. 6 Jetty,
Circular Quay, tel: (02) 9206-
6666. Cruise the harbour while
you enjoy excellent cuisine.
**Jordan's Seafood
Restaurant**, Darling Harbour,
tel: (02) 9281-3711. Excellent
fresh seafood.

South Coast
There is an excellent choice of
restaurants due in part to the
large multicultural population.
**The Lagoon Seafood
Restaurant**, Stuart Park,
North Wollongong, tel: (042)
26-1677. One of Wollongong's
most popular restaurants,
offering fresh seafood with
magnificent views.

Charcoal Tavern, 18 Regent
St, Wollongong, tel: (042)
29-7298. An innovative and
popular restaurant housed
in an old federation building
offering excellent atmosphere
and fine food.

Southern Highlands
Most of the restaurants in
the Southern Highlands are
located in the Berrima and
Bowral town centres.
Tearooms and brasseries
offer simple, wholesome
food. Resorts and hotels
have their own restaurants
and are usually licensed.

Blue Mountains
The **Visitors Information
Centre** offers the informative
Blue Mountains Wonderland
magazine which has a wide
selection of dining facilities.
Most motels and guesthouses
have their own dining rooms.
Arjuna Restaurant,
Cliff Dr, Katoomba, tel:
(047) 82-4662. Tandoori and
Indian cuisine with spectacular
mountain views.
The Fork 'n' View,
Leura Falls, Leura, tel: (047)
82-1164. Fabulous views
over the Jamison Valley
and international cuisine.
Sirens Restaurant,
194 Great Western Hwy,
Blackheath, tel: (047) 87-6111.
Contemporary Australian
cuisine served in landscaped
gardens in summer and in a
beautiful turn-of-the-century
dining room in winter.

Sydney at a Glance

Western Districts

Panthers Resort, Mulgoa Rd, Penrith, tel: (047) 21-7700. This resort offers coffee shops, restaurant and bar facilities.

Parkroyal Parramatta, 30 Phillips St, Parramatta, tel: (02) 685-0333. Elegant licensed restaurant offering a wide selection of food.

Central Coast

The Gallery Restaurant BYO, Terrigal Sailing Club, The Haven, tel: (043) 85-1863. An elegant restaurant which has spectacular views over the Pacific Ocean.

Swells Fish Cafe, 100 The Esplanade, Terrigal, tel: (043) 84-6466. Specializes in fresh local seafood.

The Karabee Floating Restaurant, Gosford Waterfront, Gosford, tel: (043) 24-2733. Floating restaurant with both indoor and outdoor dining facilities.

SHOPPING

Sydney's central business district is a mixture of specialist shops and large department stores. Free publications are available in most of the large hotels and at tourist information centres. These brochures offer shopping advice. The Rocks Chamber of Commerce publishes *The Rocks Directory* – a brochure which suggests shops in the Rocks area – and *A Guide to Buying Opals in Sydney*.

Double Bay, a well-known shopping area in Sydney's eastern suburbs, publishes a brochure and has a shopping information line for people eager to explore the area, tel: (02) 9388-8205.

Queen Victoria Building publishes a brochure which describes most of the shops in the complex.

The *Best Visitors Guide – The Harbour Connection*, a 152-page free brochure, has 40 pages on shopping in Sydney. There is even a shopping tour company called **Shopping Spree Tours** (tel: (02) 9360-6220, toll free 1800 625 969), offering hosted shopping tours.

TOURS AND EXCURSIONS

Sydney

AAT Kings has an extensive range of one- and two-day tours. 24-hour booking service, tel: (02) 9252-2788, fax: 9252-3009.

Australian Pacific Tours offer a wide range of coach tours from Sydney. The most popular is the daily tour to the Blue Mountains. 24-hour booking service, tel: (02) 13-1304, fax: 9247-2052.

Clipper Gray Line has a wide range of coach tours to most areas around Sydney. 24-hour booking service, tel: (02) 9241-3983.

Matilda Harbour Cruises depart four times a day from Darling Harbour. Luncheon cruise offers steak and seafood BBQ, tel: (02) 9264-7377.

Captain Cook Cruises offer a wonderful look at Sydney Harbour. Tickets are valid all day, so you can get off and explore. Departs from Circular Quay, tel: (02) 9206-1111.

Sydney Harbour Seaplanes offer a view of the harbour that is quite unique. The planes take off and land in the harbour, tel: (02) 9918-7472.

See Sydney from the back of a Harley Davidson with **Eastcoast Motorcycle Tours**. Also travel further afield, northern beaches and Blue Mountains. tel: (02) 9545-4321.

The New South Wales Government Tourist Travel Centre, Castlereagh St, has a large range of tour and excursion brochures and information. They can make bookings for you. tel: (02) 231-4444.

South Coast

Australian Pacific Tours, 24hr booking service, tel: 13 1304, fax: (02) 9247-2052.

FJ Tours, tel: (02) 9637-4466.

Custom Motorcycle Tours, tel: (042) 94-9096, toll free 018 029 903.

The Wollongong Visitors Centre, 93 Crown St, tel: (042) 28-0300.

Southern Highlands

Southern Highlands Discoverer, tel/fax: (048) 69-1888.

Bowral Coaches, tel: (048) 68-2827, fax: 68-2686.

Sydney at a Glance

Southern Highland Motorcycle Tours, tel: (048) 62-2978 or 61-4553.

Blue Mountains
AAT Kings, 24hr booking service, tel: (02) 9252-2788, fax: 9252-3009.
Australian Pacific Tours, 24hr booking service, tel: 13 1304, fax: (02) 9247-2052.
Clipper Gray Line, 24hr booking service, tel: (02) 9241-3983.

Central Coast
AAT King's, 24hr booking service, tel: (02) 9252-2788, fax: 9252-3009.
Great Sights South Pacific, 24-hour booking service, tel: (02) 9241-2294.
Both of the tour companies listed above offer a day tour of the Hawkesbury River, Old Sydney Town and Australian Reptile Park.

USEFUL CONTACTS

Sydney Information Booth, Martin Place – a conveniently located information booth which can answer most questions about Sydney and its surrounds. It has a large assortment of pamphlets and brochures which can come in handy; tel: (02) 9235-2424.
The Rocks Visitors Centre, 106 George St, The Rocks, tel: (02) 9255-1788.
Travellers Information, International Terminal Sydney Airport, tel: (02) 9669-5111.

Manly Visitors Information Bureau, South Steyne, Manly Beach, tel: (02) 9977-1088.
Quayside Booking Centre, Jetty 2, Circular Quay, tel: (02) 9247-5151.
YHA Membership & Travel Centre, 422 Kent St, tel: (02) 9261-1111.
National Parks and Wildlife Service, Cadman's Cottage, 110 George St, tel: (02) 9247-8861.
Government Department – Passport Information, 255 Pitt St, tel: 13 1232.

HOSPITALS
St Luke's, 18 Roslyn St, Potts Point, tel: (02) 9356-0200.
St Margaret's, 433 Bourke St, tel: (02) 9333-4000.
Sydney and Sydney Eye Hospital, Macquarie St, tel: (02) 9382-7111.
Travellers Medical & Vaccination Centre, tel: (02) 9221-4799 (information) or 9221-7133 (appointments).

EMERGENCY
Ambulance, **Fire**, **Police**, tel: 000

Southern Highlands
Visitors Information Centre, Hume Hwy, Mittagong, tel: (048) 71-2888.

Blue Mountains
Visitors Information Centre: Great Western Hwy, Glenbrook; Echo Point, Katoomba, tel: (047) 39-6266, fax: 39-6787.

Western Districts
Windsor Visitor Information Centre, cnr Windsor Rd & Groves Ave, tel: (045) 77-5915.
Penrith Information Centre, 250 High St, tel: (047) 32-7671.

Central Coast
Visitor Information Centre: Terrigal, Lagoon Tea House; **Rotary Park**, Terrigal Dr; **Gosford**, 200 Mann St; **The Entrance**, Marine Parade; **Toukley & Districts**, Wallarah Park, Gorokan.

Ring toll free 008 806 258 or tel: (043) 85-4430 for all of the visitor information centres listed above. *See also* Tourist Information in the **Travel Tips** Section on p. 122 of this book.

SYDNEY	J	F	M	A	M	J	J	A	S	O	N	D
AVERAGE TEMP. °F	73	73	72	66	63	57	54	57	61	64	68	72
AVERAGE TEMP. °C	23	23	22	19	17	14	12	14	16	18	20	22
HOURS OF SUN DAILY	8	7	7	6	6	6	7	8	8	8	8	8
RAINFALL ins.	4	4.5	5	5	5	5	4	3	3	3	3	3
RAINFALL mm	104	117	135	129	121	131	100	81	69	79	82	78
DAYS OF RAINFALL	12	12	13	12	12	12	10	10	10	11	11	12

Travel Tips

Tourist Information

The Australian Tourist Commission, in Sydney and major international cities, provides material free of charge.

All areas around Sydney have information centres which are central and clearly marked, and supply maps, brochures and other information. Open 09:00–17:00 weekdays, and on Saturday mornings.

Sydney: The Travel Centre of NSW, 19 Castlereagh St, Sydney NSW 2000, tel: (02) 9231-4444.

Blue Mountains: Glenbrook Visitor Information Centre, Great Western Hwy, Glenbrook NSW 2773, tel: (047) 39-6266. Echo Point Information Centre, Echo Point, Katoomba NSW 2780, tel: (047) 39-6266.

Southern Highlands: Tourist Information Centre in the park Hume Hwy, Mittagong NSW 2575, tel: (048) 71-2888.

South Coast: Wollongong Tourist Information Centre, 93 Crown St, Wollongong NSW 2500, tel: (042) 28-0300. Kiama Tourist Information Centre, Blowhole Point, Kiama NSW 2533, tel: (042) 32-3322 and toll free 1800 803 897.

Western Suburbs:

Macarthur Country Information Centre, Cnr Hume Hwy and Congressional Dr, Liverpool NSW 2170, tel: (02) 9821-2311. Windsor Tourist Information Centre, Cnr Windsor Rd & Groves Ave, Windsor NSW 2756, tel: (045) 77-2310 Penrith Tourist Information Centre, 250 High St, Penrith NSW 2750, tel: (047) 32-7671.

Central Coast: Central Coast Tourism, Gosford, 200 Mann St, Gosford NSW 2250, tel: (043) 25-2835.

Central Coast Tourism, Tuggerah Lakes, Marine Parade, The Entrance NSW 2261, tel: (043) 32-9282. Central Coast Tourism, Toukley, Wallarah Park, Gorokan NSW 2263, tel: (043) 92-4666. Central Coast Tourism, Terrigal, Terrigal Dr, Terrigal NSW 2260, tel: (043) 85-4074.

The National Parks and Wildlife Service provide material for areas under their jurisdiction. The National Trust offer free walking guides. The NRMA has free maps for members of affiliated organizations. NRMA, 151 Clarence St, Sydney NSW 2000, tel: (02) 9260-9222.

Entry Requirements

To enter Australia a valid passport is required and, unless you are a New Zealander, you will need a visa – obtained in advance from an Australian consular office abroad or, if you are an American travelling by Qantas, from the airline's offices in Los Angeles or San Francisco.

Short-stay visas (up to three months) are free, and **long-stay visas** (up to six months) carry a small charge of A$35 as do multiple-entry visas. Extensions requested from within Australia can be costly. Also, the amount of time you plan to spend is not entirely at your own discretion. Embassy officials might limit your time. A return ticket and 'sufficient funds' are also required.

A Working Holiday Maker – for 'young' people (usually 18 to 26) from Ireland, the UK, the Netherlands, Canada and Japan – is available from the country of origin, valid for up to one year and costs about A$145. It permits casual employment (meaning you may work for three of the 12 months). Fruit-picking is one of the most common, short-term job prospects.

Visa extensions can take a while to obtain, so apply early. A A$35 fee must be paid up-front and may not be refundable at all.

Customs

Australian Customs carry out random searches at international airports for weapons (even if they are ceremonial), drugs and contraband. International passengers must fill out a Customs Declaration, which enquires about the importation of natural products such as leather, feathers, food and timber, and requires visitors to state whether they have visited a farm prior to travel. The country has avoided flora and fauna problems common in other parts of the world and customs are eager to keep foreign diseases and pests at bay. The **Duty Free** allowance only applies to people over the age of 18. The limits are 250 cigarettes or 250g (8.5 oz) of cigars or tobacco, 1 litre (35 fl oz) of wine or spirits and gifts to the value of A$400. Amounts exceeding these are permitted but carry an import duty payable on arrival. Rates vary.

Health Requirements

Most visitors do not need vaccinations or immunizations. If you come from a country, or recently visited a country, where there is an incidence of cholera, smallpox or similar contagious diseases check with the local Australian embassy or consulate. Health certificates may be required. Australia has no contagious diseases which need to be vaccinated against.

Getting There

By Air: Book well in advance, particularly if you wish to travel at major holiday times (*see* Public Holidays on p. 125).

Sydney airport is the country's major airport and this can mean delays with landing, customs and immigration. Domestic airlines and overseas carriers use Kingsford Smith Airport.

Buses provide transport into the city and a private bus line serves major hotels (*see also* At a Glance on p. 116). You will need A$25 for **departure tax**.
By Road: Sydney and environs are easily accessible by public transport; but hire a car if you want the freedom to explore further. There are plenty of car rental agencies (with a range of prices and short-term specials), so investigate options. The major companies – Avis, Hertz, Budget – operate at Sydney Airport. A valid driving licence is essential and applicants usually must be over 21.

What to Pack

Sydney has long hot summers and generally mild winters. The Blue Mountains can drop below freezing during the winter nights, with brisk wintry days. The Central Coast is about 5C° (9F°) warmer than Sydney in winter. The South Coast and Western Suburbs are similar to Sydney. People dress informally, though 'smart casual' wear is often required after dark at theatres and more sophisticated hotels and restaurants. Beach wear is acceptable only on the beach, in pubs and fast-food outlets; casual clothing is customary in most places.

For summer (October to April) pack light clothes and a hat. It can get cool at night. Sydney often has summer rains so take an umbrella. In winter, a lightweight coat and warm clothes are usually required – especially for the Blue Mountains.

Money Matters

Banks are open 09:30–16:30, Monday–Thursday (17:00 on Fridays), but hours in the city centre can be 08:00–18:00, Monday–Friday. Building societies are often open longer.

Traveller's cheques are most readily dealt with, particularly if in Australian dollars, and have a better exchange rate than foreign currency. But all banks will readily change both, albeit with varying charges. A passport is usually sufficient proof of identity. Credit cards are widely used (except in remote areas or smaller shops) and are preferred by car rental agencies.

There are a 100 cents to the Australian dollar. Coins come in 5c, 10c, 20c, 50c, A$1 and A$2 and notes in A$5, A$10, A$20, A$50 and A$100. Any amount of money can be taken in and out of the country, but for more than A$5000 you must complete a report form.

Visitors should open a cash-card account with a major bank, allowing access to automatic tellers, which are widespread and 24hr. You can withdraw A$400–A$2000 a day and the card can be used to make calls in special booths throughout the country. They are also linked to the EFTPOS system which can allow you to pay for goods and services in certain stores.

Tipping: Tipping is not standard practice in Australia. You may wish to add an 10% to a restaurant bill, but it is not mandatory. Restaurant prices carry no extra taxes or service charges, and food is plentiful, of high quality and cheap, although manufactured goods tend to be more expensive.

Accommodation

The NRMA has a comprehensive guide to accommodation across Australia, with a lengthy section on Sydney – with star-ratings and up-to-date information. It can be bought from NRMA outlets (see p. 122).

Eating Out

Sydney has a variety of eateries (restaurants, motels, hotels, cafés) while smaller centres in the area have a more limited range. The annual *Good Food Guide* offers many suggestions and recommendations. Visitors may find food from all over the world – or choose from McDonald's, Kentucky Fried Chicken, Pizza Hut and local cafés for quick and cheap food (see also p. 118). Produce is fresh and prices are reasonable – particularly when compared to European prices.

Transport

By Air: Sydney is Australia's major airport. A large number of carriers fly to from Europe Southeast Asia, Africa, South America, North America and the Pacific Islands. Telephone numbers for the various carriers may be found in the local phone directories or Telstra enquiries on 013.

By Road: Sydney and environs are easily accessible by public transport, however hiring a car is worthwhile if you want to explore further and have the freedom of your own timetable. There are a large number of car rental agencies, both local and international. Competition means a range of prices and short-term specials, the options are worth investigating. The major companies – such as Avis, Hertz and Budget – operate at Sydney Airport. They differ little on typical round-the-city rentals but special offers begin to emerge with less typical and longer-term deals. Be aware that, while limited kilometre rates are the norm around the city, country and remote driving incurs a higher flat rate plus a charge per kilometre – and do not forget insurance! Smaller companies may often prove to be cheaper. The best source of information is a copy of the *Yellow Pages* (the Telstra telephone Business Directory) which will list all the car rental companies in the local area. A valid driving licence is essential and applicants usually must be over 21.

Buses: Bus services to and from Sydney are frequent and efficient, taking the traveller to most places – in comfort. But distances are vast and bus travel can be time consuming: Sydney to Melbourne, for example, takes 13 hours. For further details, contact Bus Australia (tel: (02) 9261-1888) or Greyhound/Pioneer (tel: (02) 9286-8600).

Trains: There is an extensive railway system in NSW called Countrylink. Interstate travel can also be booked, tel: (02) 9217-8812 or toll free 008 043 126.

Business Hours

These are 08:30 or 09:00 until 17:00 or 17:30, Monday to Friday; 09:00–13:00, Saturday, with late-night shopping on Thursday and/or Friday – shops close at 20:00 or 21:00. But these hours vary from centre to centre. Some shops stay open until 17:00 on a Saturday and some, in major centres, open on Sundays. Major supermarkets stay open longer in more densely populated areas. Corner shops, milk bars, delis and city bookshops also open for extended trading.

CONVERSION CHART		
FROM	**TO**	**MULTIPLY BY**
Millimetres	Inches	0.0394
Metres	Yards	1.0936
Metres	Feet	3.281
Kilometres	Miles	0.6214
Kilometres square	Square miles	0.386
Hectares	Acres	2.471
Litres	Pints	1.760
Kilograms	Pounds	2.205
Tonnes	Tons	0.984
To convert Celsius to Fahrenheit: x 9 ÷ 5 + 32		

ROAD SIGNS

Sydneysiders drive on the left hand side of the road and road signs conform with standard international regulations. All information about travelling around Sydney can be obtained from the NRMA . They have a wide range of maps, information on road rules and details about road signs.

Time Difference

Sydney is 10 hours ahead of Greenwich Mean Time, which means that when it is midday at GMT, it is 22:00 in Sydney, but varies in summer by 1 hour because of daylight saving.

Communications

Post Offices are open 09:00–17:00, Monday–Friday. They provide comprehensive postal services, and lettergram and international telegram facsimile transmission. Public telephones, particularly in rural areas, are located near the Post Office. Overseas postal rates are quite high. Some suburban Post Offices and those in the larger malls are open on Saturday.

Electricity Supply

The electrical current in Sydney is 220–240 volts AC. The local plug-and-socket system uses three pins. These are not the same as those in Britain, and only top hotels tend to have appropriate converters. Decent hardware stores may carry adaptors but, failing this, an Australian plug could be fitted.

Weights and Measures

Australia adopted the metric system in the 1960s. Distances are measured in kilometres, petrol and drinks in litres and millilitres, the temperature in centigrade, and food in grams and kilograms.

Health Precautions

Sydney offers high standards of hygiene and safe food and drinking water, so special precautions should not be necessary. No vaccinations are required unless some time has been spent in an infected country in the previous two weeks, but immunization is always a good idea if your international itinerary is broad.

When walking in the bush be sure to wear boots, thick long socks and long trousers and be careful about putting your hand into holes. Ticks and leeches are common so check your body thoroughly. Ticks can be dangerous, remove them with kerosene or methylated spirits (take care not to break the body off leaving the head inside your body). Leeches can be removed with salt or heat.

The chance of being attacked stung or bitten by venomous wildlife is very remote but, if a poisonous snake or spider should bite, try to stay calm, wrap the area in a tight bandage, as you would with a sprained ankle (*do not* use a tourniquet or suck out the poison), attach a splint to the limb, keep very still and send for medical help.

A similar procedure applies to poisonous marine life. Sea wasps are a deadly type of

PUBLIC HOLIDAYS

Sydneysiders commonly take their holidays during the school summer vacation, roughly 16 December –1 February. The Easter holiday usually lasts 10 days, while the winter holiday lasts for two weeks in July. There is a spring holiday from the last week of September to the second week of October. The major holidays include:

1 January • New Year's Day
26 January • Australia Day
Good Friday • (variable)
Easter Monday • (variable)
25 April • Anzac Day
10 June • Queen's birthday
25 December •
Christmas Day
26 December •
Boxing Day

jellyfish which sting, causing telltale welt marks. Douse the wound with vinegar and don't remove the stingers. Do not swim in unprotected waters.

Respect **fire bans** (broadcast on radio) and be careful with cigarette butts and broken glass which can ignite bushfires in hot, dry weather. If caught in a fire, head for a clearing (avoid dense tree growths). If in a car, get off the road, get under the dashboard and cover yourself, preferably with a woolly blanket.

If you are bushwalking or camping, be sure to leave an itinerary with friends and go prepared for the possibility of getting lost. Remember that nights can be freezing despite the day temperature. The intense sun, however, could be a problem. Sydney has a high skin cancer rate so be sure, if you are spending any length of time in its glare, to apply sun cream and to wear a broad-brimmed hat and a shirt with a collar and, preferably, long sleeves.

Health Services

Australia offers free service at public hospitals to its own citizens and permanent residents, and has universal health care under **Medicare** system. This covers most or all of the cost of visiting a general practitioner, depending largely on whether the doctor uses bulk-billing practices. But these services only extend to citizens of the United Kingdom and New Zealand. Visitors have to pay in full and up-front for dental treatment, ambulance charges and medicines. The cost of an unsubsidized, standard visit to a doctor is about A$35, but serious illness can be much more expensive. Traveller's insurance covering medical care and medicines is therefore highly recommended. A personal basic medical kit could also be a good idea.

Personal Safety

New South Wales is a benign community. Sydney is Australia's largest city and inevitably, like any large city, it has its fair share of crime. Common sense is necessary. Be sensible in Kings Cross and around Oxford Street. They are perfectly safe areas but people have been known to be beaten up and robbed. There are over 12,000 police in the state. In 1992–93 there were 110 homicides (1.9 per 100,000 people) and 4513 sexual assaults (75.7 per 100,000) throughout NSW.

Emergencies

The number for emergencies is **000** – for the police, ambulance and other emergency services. Crisis hotlines and interpreter services are listed at the front of the *White Pages* of the telephone directory. Condoms are available at chemists, some all-night stores and at vending machines in the toilets of many hotels and universities. The pill is only available on prescription which requires a visit to a doctor.

Directories list emergency services and facilities in the front section of the book.

Etiquette

Australia is generally an informal society. City businessmen still dress in suits and ties, but it is common in rural and suburban areas to find a high level of informality. Some hotels, clubs and restaurants have **dress codes**, but this is usually to ensure that people do not arrive in shorts and a singlet during the evening. Sydneysiders will happily tell you what is considered appropriate.

For more information on **tipping** service-providers, *see* Money Matters on p. 124.

Language

Australians speak English as their first language. While the country is committed to multiculturalism – which, on one level, means that most major organizations will have translators and interpreters – in suburban and regional areas people who do not speak English will have some difficulty. Telstra offers an interpreter service. Telephone numbers are available in the front of the *White Pages*.

Australian English inevitably has a number of local variations. People who wish to investigate Australian English further, should read *Aussie Talk: The Macquarie Dictionary of Australian Colloquialisms* (1984) published by the Macquarie Library, Sydney.

GOOD READING

Works of fiction set in and around Sydney include:
• Ruth Park (1948) *The Harp in the South*, Penguin, London.
• D.H. Lawrence (1923) *Kangaroo*, Penguin, London.
• Christina Stead (1944) *For Love Alone*, Angus & Robertson, Sydney.
• Kenneth Slessor (1939) *Selected Poems*, Angus & Robertson, Sydney.
Non-fiction works include:
• Cyril Pearl (1958) *Wild Men of Sydney*, Angus & Robertson, Sydney.
• Jan Morris (1992) *Sydney*, Viking-Penguin, London.
• Robert Hughes (1987) *The Fatal Shore*, Pan, London.
• Bruce Elder (1988) *Blood on the Wattle: The Massacres and Maltreatment of Aborigines since 1788*, National Books, Sydney.

INDEX